Briefe an den Orientalisten Julius Klaproth (1783–1835) von britischen Gelehrten: George Thomas Staunton, Viscount Kingsborough und William Huttmann

Herausgegeben von

Hartmut Walravens

BoD

Umschlagillustration:
Mitchelstown Castle, der Sitz von Viscount Kingsborough. Ansicht aus John Preston Neale: *Views of the seats of noblemen and gentlemen, in England, Wales, Scotland and Ireland.* (London 1819–1823).

ISBN 978-3-7526-6761-5

© 2021 by Hartmut Walravens

Bibliografische Information der Deutschen Nationalbibliothek:
Die Deutsche Nationalbibliothek
verzeichnet diese Publikation in der Deutschen Nationalbibliografie; detaillierte
bibliografische Daten sind im Internet über *dnb.dnb.de* abrufbar.

Herstellung und Verlag: BoD – Books on Demand, Norderstedt

Inhalt

Vorbemerkung

Der vorliegende Band faßt einige weitere Mosaiksteine zur Klaprothforschung zusammen, nämlich Briefe von drei Persönlichkeiten an Julius Klaproth; sie haben zweierlei gemeinsam:
- sie waren in Großbritannien tätig
- und ihre Briefe befinden sich heute in der Sammlung Klaproth im St. Petersburger Archiv der Akademie der Wissenschaften.

Der erste von Ihnen, George Thomas Staunton (26. Mai 1781–10. Aug. 1851) hatte seinen Vater auf der britischen Gesandtschaftsreise an den chinesischen Hof begleitet und dabei Chinesisch gelernt. Er ist durch mehrere Übersetzungen aus dem Chinesischen hervorgetreten.

Der zweite, Edward King, Viscount Kingsborough (16. Nov. 1795–27. Febr. 1837), aber meist als Lord Kingsborough bezeichnet, hatte das große Verdienst, die chinesische Grammatik des Jesuitenpaters Joseph Henri de Prémare, die als Manuskript kursierte und aus der sowohl Étienne Fourmont wie auch Jean Pierre Abel Rémusat ihre Grammatiken geschöpft hatten, auf eigene Kosten drucken zu lassen und damit allgemein zugänglich zu machen. Sein Hauptwerk aber war die stupende Publikation *Antiquities of Mexico* (9 Bände), zu der er durch die Forschungen Alexander von Humboldts angeregt wurde und auf die er einen beträchtlichen Teil seines Vermögens verwendete.

Der dritte, William Huttmann (9. März 1792–3. Okt. 1844), ein vielseitiger Orientalist, Autodidakt, der sich besonders mit dem Chinesischen und Mandschu beschäftigte, war zeitweise als Sekretär der (Royal) Asiatic Society tätig, ist aber auf Grund unglücklicher Lebensumstände wenig bekannt. Er gab den Anstoß zur Gründung der Royal Geographical Society.

Die Originale der im Folgenden veröffentlichten Briefe befinden sich, wie gesagt, in der St. Petersburger Filiale des Archivs der Russischen Akademie der Wissenschaften (Санкт-Петербургский филиал Российской Академии Наук)

fond 783, op. 2, Nr. 88 (Staunton)
fond 783, op. 2, Nr. 47 (Kingsborough)
fond 783, op. 2, Nr. 25 (Huttmann)

Hier seien kurz einige *neuere* Beiträge zur Klaproth-Forschung verzeichnet:

Vom Herausgeber
Katalog der chinesischen und mandjurischen Bücher der Bibliothek der Akademie der Wissenschaften in St. Petersburg von Julius Klaproth. Zum ersten Mal aus dem Manuskript herausgegeben.
Berlin: C. Bell 1988. V, 45 S. 4° (Ch'ing-wen tsung-hui 1.)
Erstausgabe.

Von der notwendigen Unterdrückung der deutschen Universitäten. Der Berliner Universalgelehrte Julius Klaproth und die Königliche Bibliothek.
Jahrbuch Preußischer Kulturbesitz 31.1995, 225-249
Erstausgabe.

Julius Klaproth (1783–1835). Leben und Werk.
Wiesbaden: Harrassowitz 1999. X, 230 S.
(Orientalistik Bibliographien und Dokumentationen 3.)
Darin Verzeichnung weiterer Literatur über Klaproth.

Julius Klaproth (1783–1835): Briefe und Dokumente.
Wiesbaden: Harrassowitz 1999. 235 S.
(Orientalistik Bibliographien und Dokumentationen 4.)
      Deutsche Übersetzung des Confucius
      Quid non audebis perfida lingua loqui!
      Von den deutschen Universitäten und ihrer nothwendigen Unterdrückung
      Vorwort zum Vaterlandsfreund
      Ehrenrettung Stephan Fourmonts
      Lettre à M. Auguis
      Über Jean Potocki's Archipel in dem nördlichen Theile des gelben Meeres
      Die Russische Gesandtschaft nach China im Jahre 1805. S. 187–203
      Aufnahme der russischen nach Peking bestimmten Gesandtschaft in der Mongolei.
      Aus dem Tagebuche eines russischen Beamten, der dieselbe begleitete. [*Das
      Ausland* 1828]

*Zur Geschichte der Ostasienwissenschaften in Europa. Abel Rémusat (1788-1832) und
das Umfeld Julius Klaproths (1783–1835).*
Wiesbaden: Harrassowitz 1999. 183 S.
(Orientalistik Bibliographien und Dokumentationen 5.)
      J. P. Abel Rémusat (1788–1832) – Biobibliographie
      Paul Schilling von Canstadt (1786–1837)
      Heinrich Kurz (1805–1873)
      Pierre François Mourier (1746–1836)
      Adelbert von Chamisso (1781–1838), Augusta Klaproth (1785–1856) und August
      von Varnhagen von Ense (1785–1858)
      Julius Klaproth und die Société asiatique
      Antoine Jean Saint Martin (1791–1832)
      Karl Friedrich Neumann (1798–1870)

Siebold and Klaproth – a «literary friendship»?
EAJRS Newsletter 9.2002, 13–18

Julius Klaproth (1783-1835): *Briefwechsel mit Gelehrten, großenteils aus dem Akade-
miearchiv in St. Petersburg.*
Wiesbaden: Harrassowitz 2002. XVII, 216 S. ISBN 3-447-04596-8
(Orientalistik Bibliographien und Dokumentationen 18.)
      Die Korrespondenten waren S. S. Uvarov, Heinrich Kurz, Samuel Butler, Schilling
      von Canstadt, Ladislaus Endlicher, Christian Martin Frähn, E. F. Jomard, Stanislas
      Julien, Philipp Fr. von Siebold, Altenstein, K. F. Neumann, Heinrich Berghaus,
      Nikolaus Fuß, H. H. Wilson, Jan Potocki und Carl Ritter.

Notes on the early history of tangram in Germany.
Cubism for fun 72. 2007
Erstausgabe.

Julius Klaproth – his life and works; with special emphasis on Japan.
Japonica Humboldtiana 10.2006, 177–191

J. Klaproth: Qi qiao tu hebi (Composing pictures from seven pieces)
Piśmennye pamjatniki Vostoka (St. Petersburg) 2 (7).2007, 21–36

Julius Klaproth, Stanislas Julien et les débuts de la sinologie européenne.
Idées de la Chine au XIXe siècle entre France et Allemagne. Paris: Indes Savantes 2014,
145–155

Julius Klaproth, Stanislas Julien und die Anfänge der europäischen Sinologie.
Mitteilungsblatt DCG 55.2012, 51–58

Schilling von Canstadt and his correspondence with Julius Klaproth in the IOM.
WMO 2019:2, 105–143

*Julius Klaproths (1783–1835) Briefe an den Orientalisten und Erfinder Paul Ludwig
Schilling von Canstadt (1786–1837).* Samt Schreiben an den Sinologus Berolinensis
sowie Ergänzungen zum Schriftenverzeichnis Klaproths.
Norderstedt: BoD 2020. 100 S.

Stanislas Julien (1797–1873): *Wissenschaftliche Korrespondenz über China mit Schilling
von Canstadt, Klaproth, Endlicher, Gabelentz, und A. von Humboldt.*
Norderstedt: BoD 2021. 110 S.

Von Frieder Sondermann
Ernst F. Sondermann: Julius von Klaproths Briefe an Joseph von Hammer.
Tôhoku gakuin daigaku kyôyôgakubu ronshû 東北学院大学教養学部論集 148.2007,
19–53

Frieder Sondermann: Heinrich Julius Klaproth (1783-1835) und Johann Caspar Horner
(1774–1834) über Kontakte zwischen Europa und Asien. *Journal of human informatics*
13.2008, 59–86

Briefe von George Thomas Staunton (1781–1859) an Julius Klaproth (1783–1835)

George Thomas Staunton[1] (Salisbury 26. Mai 1781–10. Aug. 1859 London) begleitete seinen Vater, Sir George Leonard Staunton (1737–1801), der als Sekretär und Stellvertreter des Gesandten fungierte, auf der Gesandtschaftsreise von Lord Macartney nach China, 1892–1894. Als Dolmetscher wurden zwei chinesische Geistliche gewonnen, die im Seminar in Neapel ausgebildet worden waren, und die auf des Vaters Wunsch dem jungen, damals elfjährigen Staunton bereits 1792 in London vor der Abreise sowie auf der Überfahrt Unterricht im Chinesischen erteilten. Bei der Audienz beim Kaiser war Staunton dabei und durfte sogar einige Worte auf Chinesisch an den Kaiser richten. In der Folge studierte Staunton kurze Zeit in Cambridge, bevor er 1798 bei der Faktorei der British East India Company in Canton angestellt wurde. Bei dieser Tätigkeit kamen ihm seine sich ständig verbessernden Chinesischkenntnisse zugute; in der Folge wurde er Leiter der Faktorei. 1816 begleite er als „Commissioner" die Gesandtschaft von Lord Amherst nach Peking. 1817 kehrte Staunton dauerhaft nach Großbritannien zurück. In der Folge vertrat er mehrere Wahlbezirke im House of Commons.

Von seinen sinologischen Aktivitäten sind die Übersetzung von Alexander Pearsons Traktat über die Pockenimpfung (1805), des *Ta Tsing Leu Lee, being the fundamental laws, and a selection from the supplementary statutes of the penal code of China* (auf der Grundlage der Ausgabe von 1799)(1810) und der Gesandtschaftsreise des Tuliśen zu den Torguten (1821), *Narrative of the Chinese embassy to the Khan of the Tourgouths in 1712*, zu erwähnen.

G. Th. Staunton (Quelle: Wikimedia Commons)

---

1   G. C. B.: Staunton, Sir George Thomas. *Dictionary of National Biography* 18.1921/22, 1001–1002; J. L. Cranmer-Byng: The first English sinologists. *Symposium on historical, archeological and linguistic studies on Southern China, South-East Asia and the Hong Kong region.* Ed. by F. S. Drake. Hong Kong University Press 1967, 247–260.

Zusammen mit Henry Thomas Colebrooke war er 1823 Gründer der Asiatic Society (später Royal Asiatic Society), der er seine chinesische Büchersammlung (186 Werke) überließ.[2] Er gilt als der erste britische Sinologe (im modernen Sinne).

Als Orientalist bekannter als Staunton ist der Adressat der Briefe, Heinrich Julius Klaproth (Berlin 11. Okt. 1783–27. Aug. 1835 Paris), der bereits als Schüler autodidaktisch Chinesisch lernte, dann als 19jähriger seine erste Zeitschrift herausgab, 1805 an der nach China bestimmten Golovkin-Gesandtschaft teilnahm, als Adjunkt der Petersburger Akademie der Wissenschaften den Kaukasus erforschte und später als preußischer Forschungsstipendiat mit Wohnsitz in Paris ein beachtliches Werk schuf, insbesondere zu China, Japan und Zentralasien (insgesamt über 400 Publikationen, ohne Karten). Er gilt zusammen mit J. P. Rémusat (1788–1832) als Begründer der Sinologie als kritischer Wissenschaft.[3]

In den vorgelegten Briefen geht es um chinesische Bücher und Klaproths Publikationen:

Staunton kann zwei kleine von Klaproth gewünschte chinesische Texte nicht finden. Er übersendet eine kleine Publikation von Morrison & Davis sowie einen chinesischen Impftraktat. – Er nimmt die von Klaproth für sein geplantes englisches Buch über China vorgeschlagene Widmung an. Er bedauert, Klaproth nicht mehr habe sehen können, da er wegen Krankheit seiner Mutter überstürzt aus Paris habe abreisen müssen. Seine chinesischen Bücher seien so ungünstig in London gelagert, daß er sich selbst dort um Klaproths Wünsche kümmern müsse. – Er hält Verhandlungen mit chinesischen Behörden wegen des unzweckmäßigen Zeremoniells für wenig aussichtsreich; es geht hier wohl um den britisch-chinesischen Handel. Er kann die von Klaproth gewünschten Bücher in London nicht finden. Die frisch gegründete Asiatische Gesellschaft gedeiht. – Staunton will Klaproths Bücherwunschliste nach China schicken. – Er berichtet von der Ankunft einer Bücherkiste aus China, die noch auf dem Zoll liege. Laut Morrisons Mitteilungen haben die Verhandlungen mit der chinesischen Seite doch Erfolg gehabt. – Stauntons Empfehlung beim Oriental Committee habe gleichfalls Erfolg gehabt; es geht wohl um den Druck eines Buches Klaproths. Die erwähnten Bücher aus China liegen immer noch beim Zoll. – Staunton schickt chinesische Bücher an Klaproth, darunter auch Exemplare für Jouy und Levasseur, Mitglieder der Société asiatique. – Staunton ist bemüht, einen Laozi-Text für Rémusat zu finden; er drückt seine Besorgnis wegen Rémusats Krankheit aus.

Aus diesen Hinweisen geht hervor, daß Klaproth Staunton wegen seiner chinesischen Bücher sowie seiner direkten Beziehungen nach Canton schätzte. Auch der Kontakt zur Asiatic Society war ihm wichtig, deren *Asiatic Journal* regelmäßig Beiträge oder Berichte über Arbeiten Klaproths brachte.

---

2   J. L. Cranmer-Byng: Note on a collection of Chinese books presented to the Royal Asiatic Society by Sir George Thomas Staunton in 1824. *Journal of the Hong Branch of the Royal Asiatic Society* 1.1960/61, 124–126.

3   Vgl. H. Walravens: *Julius Klaproth (1783–1835). Leben und Werk.* Wiesbaden: Harrassowitz 1999. X, 230 S. (Orientalistik Bibliographien und Dokumentationen 3.); *Julius Klaproths (1783–1835) Briefe an den Orientalisten und Erfinder Paul Ludwig Schilling von Canstadt (1786–1837).* Samt Schreiben an den Sinologus Berolinensis sowie Ergänzungen zum Schriftenverzeichnis Klaproths. Norderstedt: BoD 2020. 100 S.

Übersicht[4]

1	22. Nov. 1819
2	9. Juli 1823
3	27. Jan. 1824
4	20. März 1828
5	16. Sept. 1830
6	8. Jan. 1831
7	26. Jan. 1831
8	16. Mai 1832

1

November the 22d 1819

My dear Sir

I had the pleasure of receiving your letter of the 16th by the hands of the Baron de Bülow[5] yesterday, & now send you herewith the two little Chinese works which you wish to refer to. – I am afraid that the other two works were entered by mistake in my list, as I cannot at present find them – Allow me to take the opportunity of requesting your acceptance of a little book of Translations by Mr. Morrison[6] & Mr. Davis[7], which perhaps you have not before seen;[8] and also a Chinese Tract on the Vaccine by Puankhequa[9] a Merchant of Canton. –

Wishing you most sincerely every success, in your learned and interesting pursuits,

I have the honor to be

My dear Sir

your very faithful Servt

Geo. Tho. Staunton

Mons:

Monsieur Klaproth à Paris

---

4   Die im Folgenden veröffentlichten Briefe befinden sich im Archiv der Russischen Akademie der Wissenschaften, St. Petersburg, Sammlung (fond) 783, op. 2, Nr. 88.

5   Heinrich Freiherr von Bülow (Schwerin 16. Sept. 1792–6. Febr. 1846 Berlin) folgte Wilhelm von Humboldt 1817 als Gesandtschaftssekretär nach London, dann 1819 nach Berlin. 1827 wurde er zum Gesandten in London ernannt. Vgl. Anton Ritthaler: Bülow, Heinrich Freiherr von, in: *Neue Deutsche Biographie* 2.1955, S. 734 f.

6   Robert Morrison (Morpeth 5. Jan. 1782–1. Aug. 1834 Guangzhou), Begründer der protestantischen Chinamission; Verfasser eines umfassenden chinesischen Wörterbuchs sowie Bibelübersetzer ins Chinesische. Vgl. Obituary notice of the Reverend Doctor Morrison, with a brief view of his life and labors. *Chinese Repository* 3.1835, 177–184.

7   John Francis Davis (London 16. Juli 1795–14. Nov. 1890 Henbury), Angestellter der britischen Faktorei in Canton, 1816 Teilnehmer der Gesandtschaft von Lord Amherst nach Peking; 1844–1848 Gouverneur von Hong Kong. Sinologe und Übersetzer. "Davis, John Francis," in *Dictionary of National Biography, 1901 supplement*, London: Smith, Elder, & Co. (1901) in 3 vols.; vol. 2, S. 118–119.

8   *Translations from the original Chinese, with notes.* Guangzhou: East Asia Co. Press. 1815. (mit Robert Morrison.)

9   Puankhequa – Pan Qiguan 潘启官 (Fujian 23. Juli 1714–10. Jan. 1788, Guangzhou), Besitzer eines der bedeutendsten Handelshäuser in Canton.

2
Leigh Park[10], July 9h 1823

My dear Sir
I have had the honor to receive your letter this morning and beg to assure you I feel much flattered by the honor you have done me – I shall be proud to have my name connected with a work of so much interest and importance and when has happily fallen into such able hands. The work which you purpose is in fact the chief desideratum in oriental history which still remains once completed. It is really painful in this Era of extended information and universal improvement to have no better general work on China to refer to than the heavy and antiquated compilation of Duhalde[11]. I request you will be kind enough to put down my name for five copies of your work[12], for the publication of which I shall look with impatience.

I regret that the unfortunate circumstances in which I am placed have deprived me of the pleasure of your society since your visit to the Country. I was suddenly recalled from Paris by the intelligence of the alarming illness of my revered Mother, and before I reached London she was unhappily no more.[13] – This afflicting event still disables me from entering into any society but should you prolong your stay in England for any time, I may still have the pleasure of seeing you, previous to your return to the Continent. – I shall be happy therefore to know whether you are going to Shrewsbury or not as you intended, & how long you are likely to remain with us.
I regret that my Chinese books are so placed that it is out of my power to give you access to them, until my return to London. – but I shall yet hope for an opportunity of showing them to you –
I have the honor to be
My dear Sir
your very sincere and faithful Ser^t
GeoThoStaunton

---

10   Heute ein Vorort von Havant, Hampshire (an der englischen Südküste, in der Nähe von Portsmouth).
11   *Description geographique historique, chronologique, politique, et physique de l'Empire de la Chine et de la Tartarie Chinoise,* enrichie des Cartes generales et particulieres de ces Pays, de la Carte générale & des Cartes particuliers du Thibet, & de la Corée, & ornée d'un grand nombre de Figures & de Vignettes gravées en Taille-douce. Par le P. J. B. Du Halde, de la Compagnie de Jesus. Paris: Le Mercier 1735. 4 Bde.
12   Es handelt sich hier um eine neue *Description of China,* die auch angekündigt wurde und auf Englisch in London erscheinen sollte. Das Schicksal des Buches ist mir nicht bekannt. Das Manuskript befand sich nicht im Nachlaß. Die Widmung gab Klaproth daraufhin seiner Mandschuanthologie von 1828 bei. Vgl. die Abb.
13   Lady Jane Staunton starb im Jahre 1823.

A

Sir GEORGE-THOMAS STAUNTON,

BARONET,

AUQUEL LES ÉTUDES CHINOISES, EN EUROPE,

ONT DE SI GRANDES OBLIGATIONS,

ET

QUI PROTÉGE ET ENCOURAGE,

AVEC UN ZÈLE HÉRÉDITAIRE,

LES PROGRÈS DE LA LITTÉRATURE ORIENTALE

EN ANGLETERRE.

———

HOMMAGE DE L'ESTIME DE L'AUTEUR

Widmung für G. Th. Staunton, ursprünglich vorgesehen für *Description of China*,
dann abgedruckt in *Chrestomathie mandchou* (1828)

3

17 Devonshire Street London
January 27th 1824

My dear Sir

I have had the honor to receive your letter of the 10th & note of the 13th with your "Memoires relatifs à l'Asie"[14] as far as P. 144 – for which I beg to return you my best thanks. The subject is the more interesting to me from its connection with that of the little work I published some years ago.

I am pleased to perceive that you quite agree with me in the inexpediency with the Chinese ceremonial – indeed you go further than I do, and condemn the policy of sending briberies to China, in toto; and I must myself admit that under present circumstances there is little prospect to negotiate advantageously with the local Government of Canton, which

---

14   J. Klaproth: *Mémoires relatifs à la Chine, contenant des recherches historiques, géographiques et philologiques sur les peuples de l'Orient.* Paris: Dondey-Dupré 1824. 478 S.

is better acquainted than that of Pekin, with the value of our Trade, and of our present weight in the scale of Nations.

I hope you are proceeding in your grand work upon China. I am sorry to say I do not find any work in my Chinese Collection under either of the titles you have communicated to me – and I therefore think you must have seen it in some other list than mine – I am sure our Asiatic Society of London would be happy to aid [?] your researches with any work they may possess – but I am almost sure this work is not in their collection.

I am happy to inform you that our Society[15] flourishes – we have taken a very good house for our meetings – and are now preparing our first volume for the press.
I have the honor to be with great truth
your most faithful Servt
GeoThoStaunton

4
Devonshire Street March 20th 1828

My dear Sir
My absence from London during the autumn and some accidental circumstances since that time have, I fear, made me appear very neglectful and inattentive, in not sooner acknowledging with thanks, the receipt of your obliging letter of the 3d of last October, and the accompanying very interesting volume on the "Province limitrophe entre la Russie et la Perse".[16] I hope you will kindly accept this apology, and believe that I always receive with the greatest satisfaction the valuable fruits of your researches into Eastern literature and Geography – We have had the pleasure recently, on the authority of your name & talents, of dispensing with the strictness of our ruler in the Asiatic Society of London, in order to avail ourselves of your offer to furnish us with a translation illustrated by a memoir on the obscure subject of the inscription on the Ancient Chinese Drums – a subject on which I can find hardly any notice whatever in any existing European work upon China.

I shall forward to China your catalogue of the Chinese works which were wanting in your last supply, and hope in the course of a twelvemonth to be able to procure them for you.

I shall be obliged to pass some part of this summer in Ireland, where I have some property which requires my attention – but I hope to be able to visit Paris in the autumn, in which case I shall be very happy to meet you there.
I have the honor to be
My dear Sir
your most faithful Servt
Geo Tho Staunton

I beg to enclose for your amusement a Newspaper lately established by the Americans at London –

---

15   The Royal Asiatic Society wurde 1823 mitbegründet von Staunton.
16   Klaproth: *Tableau historique, géographique, ethnographique et politique du Caucase et des provinces limitrophes entre la Russie et la Perse.* Paris: Ponthieu, Michelsen 1827. 187 S.

5

Leigh Park Havant Sept. 16 1830

I have the pleasure to inform you that I have at length had an account of a box of books sent me from Canton, containing some portion of those which you were desirous of procuring. It will be some time before they are delivered from the Custom House, and I shall not be able to unpack and examine them until my return to Town the end of October or beginning of November – but in the mean while I have to request of you to let me know what I shall do with such of the books as it may be in my power to spare you; and which I shall beg of you to do me the honor to accept in testimony of my sincere consideration.

I have recently received letters from China of the 8th of April from that distinguished Chinese scholar and excellent man Dr Morrison who mentions that all our disputes with the Government were settled, and the Trade going on as usual.

I have the honor to be

My dear Sir

your most faithful Servt

GeoThoStaunton

6

Brighton January 8th 1831

My dear Sir

I assure you that it was most gratifying to me that the Oriental Committee under the direction of Sir Gore Ouseley[17], so readily acceded to my recommendation of your care to their favor; and I sincerely trust that your interesting and valuable pursuits will not be again disturbed by similar difficulties. I had at first proposed to endeavor to raise the money by a subscription among your friends, and had put down my own name for £ 50; but it is much better and more honorable to you, that the arrangement should be the act of the Committee, which very probably had been appointed to assemble another day or two after I had received your letter. With regard to the Collection of Chinese Books I am vexed to say that they are still at the Custom house; but when I return to London next week, I shall make another effort to get them, and will then have the pleasure of sending you what I can, by the care of Mr. de Bulow the Prussian Minister.

Believe me

with great truth

My dear Sir

very faithfully yours

GeoThoStaunton

7

London Devonshire street Jan 26 1831

My dear Sir

I had the pleasure of sending yesterday to the house of His Excellency the Baron Mr. Bülow, a box and a parcel to your address, containing the following Chinese works

one copy 淵鑑類函 120 pen

---

17 Gore Ouseley (Limerick 24. Juni 1770–18. Nov. 1844 Hall Barn Park), britischer Diplomat und Orientalist. Er war 1810–1814 Botschafter in Teheran.

6 copies	康熙字典	
2 copies	廣輿記	
1 copy	通鑑綱目	120 pen
4 copies	好逑傳	
1 copy	三國誌	

I am sorry to say that the work which you particularly wish to have, has not been sent to me – 佩文韻府. My friend and correspondent Dr. Pearson[18] could not obtain a copy for less than 150 dollars which sum he refused to give, thinking it an exorbitant price.

I shall feel much obliged by your sending to Mr. Jouy[19] & Mr. Levasseur[20], each a copy of the Kang hy Dictionary & the pleasing History in my name, as Dr. Morrison to procure these works for them. –
I have another small case of books from China, but have not yet had time fully to examine it

Believe me, My dear Sir
in haste
but very faithfully yours
GeoThoStaunton

8
Devonshire street May 16th 1832

My dear Sir
I will not delay any longer to acknowledge the favor of your letter of the 23? of last month, altho my constant engagements have hitherto put it out of my power to take the necessary steps for making your executing your commission – I will however take the earliest opportunity of visiting the Library of the Royal Society, to ascertain whether they really possess the Translation of the Tao-te King to which you allude – and whether they will permit it to be copied – and lastly whether there this can be accomplished for 500 francs.

I beg you will inform our esteemed friend M. Remusat[21] that nothing would give me more pleasure than to be able to contribute to the end of his interesting literary pursuits – I was much concerned to hear of his illness, and trust that he is surely, though slowly recovering his health.

I am happy to find that you have yourself preserved your health and with [?] the prevalence of that most formidable Epidemic, the Cholera – It seems now to be generally subsiding, and I trust it will in the course of a few weeks almost entirely disappear. Here in England we have been of late so much agitated with our political discussions, that almost every other subject has been forgotten – but as the Government is apparently

---

18   Alexander Pearson (1780–1874), der Arzt der britischen Faktorei in Canton, führte dort die Pockenschutzimpfung ein. Er verfaßte darüber einen Traktat, der von G. Th. Staunton ins Chinesische (und von Klaproth ins Deutsche) gebracht wurde.

19   Jouy war Mitglied der Société asiatique und regte 1829 den Neudruck des Wörterbuchs von Basilio Brollo (1813) in einem handlichen Format an.

20   J. C. V. Levasseur war Vermessungsingenieur aus Rouen; er hatte bei Rémusat Chinesisch gelernt und lithographierte das *Zhongyong* und das *Yujiaoli*.

21   Jean Pierre Abel Rémusat (1788–1832), Arzt und erster sinologischer Lehrstuhlinhaber in Europa (Paris 1814), wurde ein Opfer der grassierenden Cholera. Vgl. H. Walravens: *Jean-Pierre Abel Rémusat (1788–1832). Zu Leben und Werk eines Wegbereiters der Ostasienwissenschaften.* Norderstedt: BoD 2020. 153 S.

reestablished in popular hands I trust we shall have more quiet and leisure for the future
I shall write you again as soon as I have any information to communicate, and always as
My dear Sir,
very faithfully yours
GeoThoStaunton

Briefe von Viscount Kingsborough (1795–1837) an den Orientalisten Julius Klaproth (1783–1835)

Edward King, Lord (eigentlich Viscount) Kingsborough (Cork 16. Nov. 1795–27. Febr. 1837 Dublin) ist wenig bekannt, und wenn dann als Mäzen, der das monumentale neunbändige Werk *Antiquities of Mexico* edierte, verfaßte, finanzierte und publizierte. Jeder dieser Bände wiegt fast dreißig Kilogramm.

> *Antiquities of Mexico: comprising fac-similes of ancient Mexican paintings and hieroglyphics, preserved in the royal libraries of Paris, Berlin and Dresden, in the Imperial library of Vienna, in the Vatican library; in the Borgian museum at Rome; in the library of the Institute at Bologna; and in the Bodleian library at Oxford. Together with the Monuments of New Spain, by M. Dupaix: with their respective scales of measurement and accompanying descriptions. The whole illustrated by many valuable inedited manuscripts, by Augustine Aglio.* 9 Bände, London 1831–1848.

Die Familie war in Irland ansässig und wohlhabend, allerdings war George King, Edwards Vater politisch tätig und ambitioniert – er baute in Mitchelstown in Cork ein Schloß im Stil von Windsor Castle, lebte verschwenderisch und war bald stark verschuldet. Der junge Edward erhielt eine gute Ausbildung, studierte kurz in Oxford (vorher wohl in Eton), machte aber keinen Abschluß. Er befreundete sich in Oxford mit dem bedeutenden Büchersammler Sir Thomas Phillips (1792–1872), mit dem er weiter im Kontakt blieb. Angeregt durch Alexander von Humboldts Arbeiten interessierte er sich für mexikanische Codices und Malereien, durchforstete die großen europäischen Sammlungen und ließ geeignete Stücke für eine Gesamtausgabe kopieren. Auch gelang es ihm, Material zu erwerben, so die Zeichnungen der Sammlung Latour Allard. Überdies finanzierte er eine Reise des Malers und Zeichners Jean Frédéric Maximilien Waldeck in Mexiko. Kingsborough konnte sein großes Werk nicht fertigstellen, denn er starb unvermittelt an Typhus, als er wegen einer vergleichsweise trivialen Schuldforderung ins Gefängnis geworfen wurde. Sein Vater stand wegen einer Geisteskrankheit zu dem Zeitpunkt unter Kuratel, sodaß Edward zwar genug Geld zur Bewirtschaftung der Güter und für seinen Lebensunterhalt, aber nicht für seine aufwendigen Liebhabereien bekam. Möglicherweise war der Gefängnisaufenthalt inszeniert, um den Kanzler zur Freigabe weiterer Mittel zu bewegen; aber das ist Vermutung. Der Vater starb zwei Jahre später, und Edward wäre dann in den Besitz eines nicht unbedeutenden Vermögens gelangt ...[22]

Wie kam es nun zu einer Verbindung zwischen Kingsborough und Julius Klaproth (1783–1835), dem vielseitigen, in Paris auf Kosten des preußischen Staates forschenden Orientalisten? Klaproth war Mitglied der (Royal) Asiatic Society, hatte London besucht, hatte britische Gelehrte in London wie auch in Paris kennengelernt, plante die Veröffentlichung eines Chinabuches in London und gab zwei Werke auf Kosten des Oriental Translation Fund heraus. Er stand mit Samuel Butler, Bischof von Lichfield, mit Sir George Thomas Staunton, William Marsden und anderen in Verbindung, und seine Arbeiten waren in britischen Orientalistenkreisen bekannt, da das *Asiatic Journal* laufend darüber berichtete, nicht zuletzt dank des rührigen Sekretärs der Asiatic Society, William Huttmann, mit dem Klaproth in dauerndem Kontakt stand. Für Klaproth war die

---

22   Sylvia D. Whitmore: Lord Kingsborough and his Contribution to Ancient Mesoamerican Scholarship: The Antiquities of Mexico. *The PARI Journal.* 9, 4. San Francisco 2009, S. 8–16.

Bekanntschaft mit einem wohlhabenden Mäzen in Hinsicht auf seine Projekte und Publikationen von großer Bedeutung.

Kingsborough fand in Klaproth einen vielseitig interessierten, gut vernetzten und außerordentlich kenntnisreichen Gelehrten auf dem Kontinent, der ihm neue Nachrichten lieferte, Kontakte anknüpfen und Arbeiten ausführen lassen und kontrollieren konnte. So spielte Klaproth eine wichtige Rolle bei der Verbesserung der Beziehungen zu Rémusat und beim Kopieren der Codices der Pariser Königlichen Bibliothek.

ANTIQUITIES OF MEXICO:

COMPRISING

FAC-SIMILES

OF

ANCIENT MEXICAN PAINTINGS AND HIEROGLYPHICS,

PRESERVED

IN THE ROYAL LIBRARIES OF PARIS, BERLIN, AND DRESDEN;

IN THE IMPERIAL LIBRARY OF VIENNA;

IN THE VATICAN LIBRARY;

IN THE BORGIAN MUSEUM AT ROME;

IN THE LIBRARY OF THE INSTITUTE AT BOLOGNA;

AND IN THE BODLEIAN LIBRARY AT OXFORD.

TOGETHER WITH

THE MONUMENTS OF NEW SPAIN,

By M. DUPAIX:

WITH THEIR RESPECTIVE

SCALES OF MEASUREMENT AND ACCOMPANYING DESCRIPTIONS.

———

THE WHOLE ILLUSTRATED BY MANY VALUABLE

Inedited Manuscripts,

By LORD KINGSBOROUGH.

THE DRAWINGS, ON STONE, BY A. AGLIO.

———

IN SEVEN VOLUMES.

VOL. II.

———

LONDON:

PRINTED BY JAMES MOYES, CASTLE STREET, LEICESTER SQUARE.

PUBLISHED BY ROBERT HAVELL, 77, OXFORD STREET;

AND

COLNAGHI, SON, AND CO. PALL MALL EAST.

———

M.DCCC.XXXI.

Übersicht[23]

1	7. 4. 1825
2	22. 7.1831
3	25. 8. 1831
4	23.10.1831
5	8. 11. 1831
6	13. 12. 1831
7	22. 12. 1831
8	28. 1. 1832
9	24. 3. 1832
10	11. 7. 1832
11	6. 8. 1832
12	1. 9. 1834 von Baradère

1

5 Grove Hackney
April 7. 1825

Dr. Morrison[24] presents his Compts to M. Klaproth & encloses an order on the Bookseller for the Number of the Dictionary which is wanting.
There are some Latin Translations of the 五經 & 四書 on the Continent if M. Klaproth could cause copies to be sent to sent on to Messrs Kingsborough for Dr. Morrison it will be esteemed a favor.

2

3. White Hall Place
July 22d 1831

Sir

I beg to apologize to you for having so long delayed replying to the letter which I had the honour of receiving from you dated Paris July the 9th, I have since received another letter which you have done me the favour of addressing to me, accompanied with some highly interesting memoirs, for which, permit me to return you my best thanks. Having already most of your published works it afforded me additional gratification to receive these memoirs directly from yourself. It certainly is an object of deeper importance than to mere literature, that the publication of the result of researches to which you have dedicated so many years, and for which you are so eminently qualified by your extensive knowledge of the languages of Asia, should not be retarded by the causes to which you have alluded in your letter to me.

---

23   Die Briefe befinden sich im Fond 783 [Klaproth], op. 2, Nr. 47 des Archivs der Russischen Akademie der Wissenschaften, St. Petersburg.

24   Robert Morrison (1782–1834), Gründer der protestantischen Chinamission. Er verbrachte die Jahre 1824–1826 in Großbritannien, wo er Mitglied der Royal Society wurde; er brachte bei dieser Gelegenheit seine chinesische Bibliothek mit nach London. Vgl. den Nekrolog in *Das Ausland* 1835, 443–444, 447–448; A. Wylie: *Memorials of Protestant missionaries to the Chinese*. Shanghae: American Presbyterian Mission Press 1867, 3–9. Seine bedeutendste Leistung ist das Chinesische Lexikon, das schnell Deguignes' Publikation von 1813 ersetzte: *A dictionary of the Chinese language, in three parts*: part the first, containing Chinese and English, arranged according to the radicals, part the second, Chinese and English arranged alphabetical, and part the third, English and Chinese, by the Rev. Rob. Macao: Printed at the Honourable East India Company Press 1815–1823.

Flattered as I necessarily must be by the proposal contained in the letter, I still am obliged to decline acceding to your wishes for reasons which it is unnecessary for me more particularly to explain, but no one will feel more anxious than myself for the speedy publication of your learned researches which I am confident will confer so much benefit in literature and sciences
I have the honor to remain Sir
Your most Obedt. Humble. Servt
Kingsborough
Allow me to request your acceptance of a copy of the Antiquities of Mexico which if you will name any bookseller in London to whose care you should wish it to be delivered. I will desire (?) the copy shall soon be sent to them.

3

3 White Hall Place
August 25th 1831

Sir
Mr. Hering of No. 9 Newman Street Oxford Street will deliver to your order the copy of the Antiquities of Mexico which you have done me the honour of accepting which I fear will not be ready before the end of next month or the beginning of October. The number of volumes which he is to send you is 7, I shall take on (?) that the eighth and ninth volumes shall be transmitted to you as soon as published.

Permit me to thank you and to say how much I shall feel flattered by your promise of sending to me the essays mentioned in your last letter which I can assume you shall on no account to show (?) to any one
I have the honour to remain Sir
Your most Obedient Humble Servant
Kingsborough

4

3 White Hall Place
October 23d 1831

Sir
I did not imagine when I last had the honour of addressing you that I should so soon have to request a personal favour of you. You are acquainted I believe with M. Rémusat Librarian of the Royal Library at Paris and Professor of Chinese. Between this gentleman and myself a misunderstanding has arisen from the following simple cause, I ventured about six years ago to request his acceptance of a snuff box which I had received from China covered with Chinese characters and made out of a sort of greenish stone. I received it as a great curiosity and monument of Chinese Antiquity from Doctor Morrison. M. Remusat to my great surprise not only thought proper to refuse this slight present but imputing a design to remunerate him for the favour of obtaining a copy of the grammar of Premare from the Royal Library (which as it cost me 100£ to have transcribed I considered no favour) accompanied his refusal with remarks to which he added a poignancy of insult by adding "J'ose me flatter qu'elles ne vous blesseront pas, mais s'il en etoit tems tout encore je voudrois qu'elles vous decidessent a vous renfermer dans les bornes d'une munificence purement literaire" and at the very time when I had offered to

him the Chinese Grammar of Premare printed at my own expense which I thought would have been highly gratifying to the Chinese professor although I am now assured I was mistaken in that supposition.[25] To his letter I did not and could not return any reply, and the correspondence on my part ceased between us. Having known [an] occasion to present a copy of the Antiquities of Mexico to the French Institute Mr. Warden informed me in the following passage of his letter dated Sept. 1st that some Mexican paintings of which I might obtain copies had lately been brought to Paris „I have informed Mr. Rich of several documents concerning Mexican Antiquities lately brought to Paris of which he might procure copies on his return to this city". I according[ly] desired Mr. Rich to apply for permission to have copies taken of these paintings and was told by him that the permission was obtained and that I had only to direct any artist I thought proper to copy them. Mr. Julien[26] on coming to London last month received a proposal from me to copy them, to which he immediately acceded requesting me to write a line to Mr. Remusat to lend him the MS for the purpose, which proposal in my answer to his note I passed over in silence and imagining that there could be no serious difficulty in the way of any copying them, merely desired him to write to me on his return to Paris, which he promised to do, and the letter which I have just received from him and which I take the liberty of enclosing to you will I assume be a sufficient apology for my addressing you on this occasion, since there is one point in it which I should wish to have explained even to the satisfaction of Mr. Remusat, and that is my apparent breach of promise in not having sent an essay of the work to the Royal Library at Paris, the reason for which omission is simply this, that the work is not yet published, and that having sent no complete copies of it to any library on the continent, or even any portion of it to the Bodleian Library at Oxford which supplied me with such valuable materials for it is a manner the most flattering on the part of some distinguished persons in that university to myself, I have not yet sent a copy to the Royal Library at Paris, the only copies which I have yet given away on the continent being one which was transmitted by me to his Majesty the King of Spain and the other which I sent to the French Institute. From the tenor of Dr. Julien's letter to me and the repulsa sordida which my application has met with at the Royal Library of Paris you might almost suppose, Sir, that a work at which I have expended so much with the sole object of adressing science, on some booksellers speculation, or at least a work of no intrinsic merit and although you have been pleased to express yourself in very complimentary terms to me of it I can not see that you know any thing of it except by rumour, since it will not be published for a month, and has never been spoken of in the reviews, I therefore cannot refrain from enclosing you a letter which I received from the

---

25 Diese Reaktion läßt sich allenfalls dadurch erklären, daß Rémusat nicht glücklich darüber war, daß nun eine breitere Öffentlichkeit feststellen konnte, daß seine Grammatik im Wesentlichen auf Prémares *Notitia* fußte. Julien bemerkte später über seinen Lehrer: „Bei der Veröffentlichung seiner Grammatik machte RÉMUSAT ganz einfach eine Abkürzung von PRÉMARE, und in seinem Vorwort wagte er zu sagen, daß die Beispiele an den Autoren überprüft worden seien, und gab zu verstehen, daß er diese Überarbeitung selbst vorgenommen habe. Früher spielte Frederic Newman [Friedrich NEUMANN](dieser mittelmäßige bayerische Sinologe) Remusat einen bösen Streich, indem er alle Seiten und Zeilen von Prémare zitierte, aus denen er seine Beispiele gezogen hatte. Als RÉMUSAT seine Grammatik veröffentlichte, hatte er fast nichts Chinesisches gelesen und als er starb (4. Juni 1832) hatte er die *Sishu* noch nicht gelesen." (Walravens: *Stanislas Julien*, 85.)

26 Stanislas Julien (1797–1873), klassischer Philologe, als Sinologe Schüler und Nachfolger von Jean Pierre Abel-Rémusat (1788–1832), der den ersten sinologischen Lehrstuhl Europas innehatte. Er wurde bei den Klassikern durch seine vorbildliche *Mengzi-Ausgabe* bekannt, übersetzte schöne Literatur, naturwissenschaftlich-technische Werke und forschte über den Buddhismus. Er war Mitglied des Instituts. Vgl. H. Walravens: Stanislas Aignan Julien – Leben und Werk. 21. Sept. 1797–14. Febr. 1873. *Monumenta Serica* 62.2014, 261–333; neuerdings: Walravens: *Stanislas Julien. Wissenschaftliche Korrespondenz über China mit Schilling von Canstadt, Klaproth, Endlicher, Gabelentz und A. von Humboldt.* Norderstedt: BoD 2021. 110 S.

Asiatic Society in London (of which I believe you are a member) which will show you the opinion which learned men in this country entertain of my exertions to throw light upon an Asian[27] portion of History to the study of which I was first led by the perusal of the writings of your illustrious countryman the Baron de Humboldt[28], whose address I think I asked you for in my last letter, but as I have not the honour of his personal acquaintance on renewed consideration I will not trouble you to send me, lest having never had any correspondence with there should be something abrupt in this mode of self introduction. So I resort to the subject of a former letter which I received from you, I must express the lively interest which I feel in the result of your researches, these which have engrossed my attention for the last three years, I must own no literary subject or scientific enquiry would inspire me with a greater desire to see its object realized, and it would give me the greatest illusion at no distant period known [?] to be [serviceable?] by any means in my sense to so useful an object, should I find that your theory upon a most important subject is not in direct opposition to my own, since known I might admire the talent and learning displayed in your researches (which I have had occasion to feel surprised at in your published works) my own opinion upon a question which may involve much religious discussion are quite made up, but in giving publicity to some researches which I have made in the 6th vol. of the Antiquities of Mexico recollecting the courtesy which I experienced in a very high quarter, I have acted upon the ancient maxim of Aristotle, who judged that truth or the attainment of truth was to be prized above all other considerations and to be preferred even to the friendship of Plato. I beg Sir that you will excuse my having addressed this very long letter to you previously to my departure from London to Ireland whither proceeding in about ten days. I should have sent you a copy of the grammar of Premare but that I dare say you have already got one, as the book has come out in a form which however little likely to gratify a thinking and critical professor will still I flatter myself be useful to the scholar who wishes to attain a knowledge of the Chinese language, and to the man of learning who is already versed in many languages since I am persuaded that if μεγα βιβλιον be μεγα κακον[29], Βιβλιον πολυτελες[30] is a much greater evil, which in the case of the Antiquities of Mexico I wish in some measure to avoid by desiring that the unbound copies of the work should be published at a price not exceeding 80 Guineas.

I have the honour to remain Sir
with the sentiments of the highest respect
Your most Obedt. Humble Servt
Kingsborough

---

27 Bezüglich der Nennung der *asiatischen* Geschichte ist zu bedenken, daß Kingsborough überzeugt war, die altamerikanischen Kulturen seien die verlorenen Stämme Israels.
28 Hier wird ein in der Fachliteratur noch bestehendes Rätsel gelöst – Kingsboroughs Interesse an amerikanischen Altertümern ging nicht auf seine Freundschaft mit Sir Thomas Phillips noch auf seine Betrachtung des Codex Mendoza in Oxford zurück, sondern auf die Schriften Alexander von Humboldts.
29 Nach Kallimachos.
30 „Luxusbuch."

5

3 White Hall Place
November 8th 1831

Sir

I feel exceedingly obliged to you for the explanation which you have given to M. Remusat, which I hope has proved satisfactory to him, and I shall on that supposition request you to present him the enclosed note, in which I ask his permission as Librarian of the Royal Library to have copies taken of the five Mexican paintings which it contains. I shall gladly avail myself of your offer to employ a proper draftsman to copy those paintings and also the painting preserved in the library of the Chamber of Deputies[31]. The mode of copying them which I should prefer as having been that which has been invariably resorted to in copying the paintings of which the facsimiles are published, and which ensures the greatest accuracy in taking the outlines, is by laying transparent paper over them of the particular kind of which I enclose you a specimen, which appears to be oiled and is extremely fine and strong – I hope that you will have received two copies of the Chinese Grammar of Premare[32] of which

---

31   Der aztekische Codex Borbonicus, in der Bibliothèque de l'Assemblée Nationale.

32   Es handelt sich wohl um die beiden bei Cordier: *Bibliotheca sinica*, 1664, erwähnten Exemplare mit dem Impressum: curâ et sumtibus Collegii anglo-sinici: Möglicherweise wurde die Formulierung geändert, da die Ausgabe ja nicht sumtibus, sondern nur cura Collegii erschien. – *Notitia linguae sinicae*. Auctore P. Premare. Malaccae: cura Academiae Anglo-Sinensis 1831. 262, 28 S. Diese Druckausgabe nennt Kingsboroughs Namen nicht. Cordier S. 1666 druckt dazu einen Auszug aus einem Brief von Kingsborough an Morrison (s.Z. in London, 8. März 1825) ab: „The Notitia Sinica, by Father Premare, the Ms. of which exists in the Royal Library of France is now transcribing; he (Lord K.) hopes that no accident will befall this copy before it reaches its destination, as it has cost him 60 guineas to have it copied out. M. Abel Remusat was the person who found, among his Chinese pupils, a person qualified for that task. This Ms. consists of 250 leaves, or 500 pages; it is written in Latin, is divised into two parts; the first of which lays down rules for the composition of Chinese in the Ancient classical style. The second, for the composition of the modern style. The justness of the rules are verified by innumerable examples taken from the most approved writers ancient and modern; hence the book abounds with Chinese Characters. M. Abel Remusat has composed an index for the whole: the labour of making that index required a length of time, and as it will be a great advantage and addition to the work, Lord Kingsborough promised that it should be duly acknowledged in the pages of the work, &c., &c. He ought now to apologize to Dr. Morrison for writing at such length to him; he has however dispatched the subjects of two or three notes in one – when completed (in a few months) the copy of Premare's work will be sent to Dr. Morrison; and he thinks the Chinese College, by the publication of a work of this learned Jesuit – confessedly the most profoundly versed in the genius of the Chinese language of the Roman Catholic Missionaries who visited China – will be doing a thing useful to the friends of science, and creditable to themselves." (gedruckt in *Memoirs of R. Morrison.* II, S. 317/318). – Hier sei noch auf zwei Manuskripte der *Notitia* hingewiesen, die Cordier in *Bibl. sin.* aus dem Nachlaß Klaproths beschrieben hat: ein vermutlich in China geschriebenes Exemplar, wohl Prémares eigenes an Étienne Fourmont gesandtes (Ms. Add. 11707), das ein caput tertium enthält: De Sinicâ urbanitate inter loquendum (fehlt in der Druckausgabe, die nach dem Ms. in der Bibliothèque nationale de France erstellt wurde); das zweite Ms. im Umfang von 394 S. (Add. 11708), das nach Landresse' Meinung von S. Julien herrührt, während Cordier es Rémusat zuschreiben will. Beide Exemplare befinden sich heute in der British Library, während Juliens Abschrift die dem Druck zugrunde lag, in den Besitz von Alexander Wylie überging. – In diesem Zusammenhang sei auf eine Auseinandersetzung zwischen Julien und Klaproth aufmerksam gemacht, in der es um den Tausch eine Teilabschrift der *Notitia* (vier Monate Arbeit) gegen eine rare Ausgabe des Daodejing ging. Dabei erwähnt Julien, daß er selbst eine „schöne vollständige Kopie der Grammatik von Prémare in 466 Seiten in folio auf doppeltem Chinapapier besitze." Die Abschrift für Lord Kingsborough wurde mit 1200 Franken honoriert. Vgl. H. Walravens: *Stanislas Julien - Wissenschaftliche Korrespondenz über China. Norderstedt* 2021.

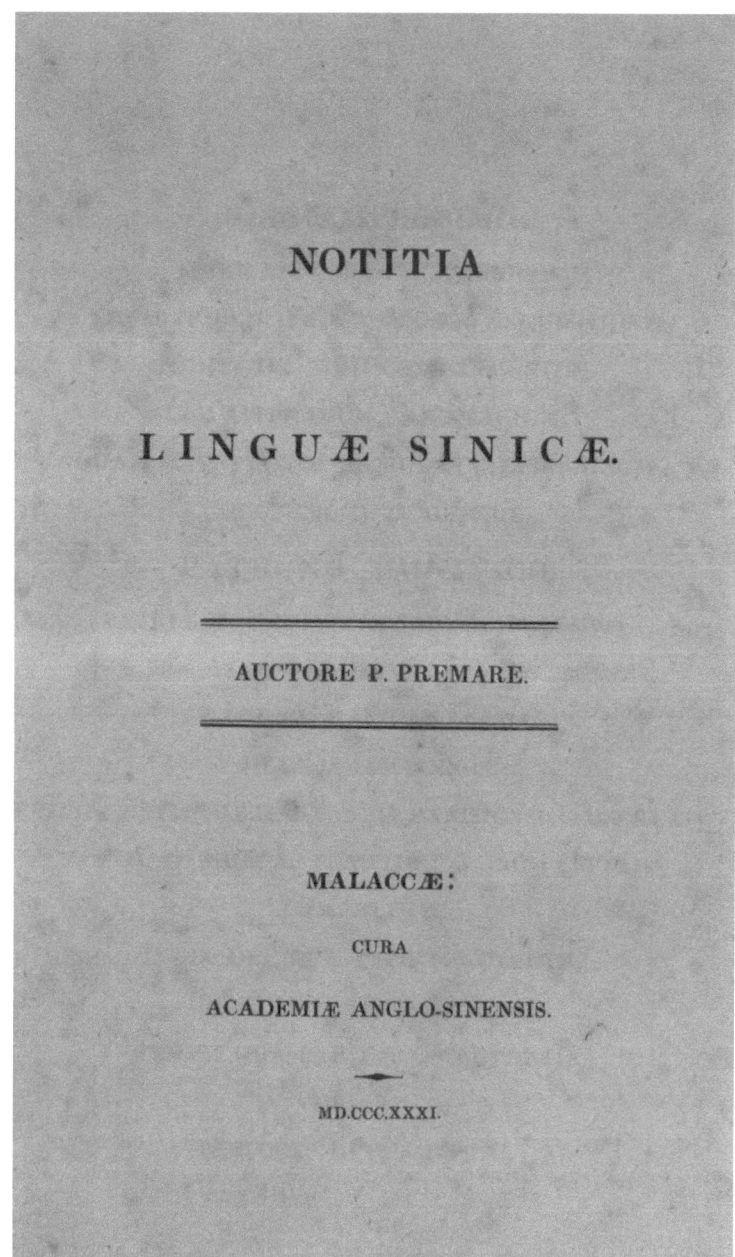

I beg your acceptance. I should esteem it a favour if you would have a specimen of a page
or two of each of the Mexican Paintings preserved in the Royal Library copied, and would
transmit me the copies to 3. White Hall Place from where they will forwarded to me to
Ireland should I have left town –
I have the honour to remain Sir
Your Obedt. Humble Servt.
Kingsborough

VIRO AMPLISSIMO

INTER PROCERES BRITANNICOS

OB ERUDITIONEM DOCTRINAMQUE EXQUISITIOREM

MULTIS DE NOMINIBUS INSIGNITO,

TAM LITERARUM ORIENTALIUM

QUAM SCIENTIARUM ARTIUMQUE LIBERALIUM

QUOCUMQUE IN GENERE

PATRONO MUNIFICO,

PATRIÆ ET ORDINIS DECORI AC PRÆSIDIO,

OPUS HOC DOCTUM, CONCINNUM, UTILISSIMUM,

E CODICE MANU EXARATO

MULTOS JAM ANNOS

SCRINIIS BIBLIOTHECÆ REGALIS PARISIENSIS ADSERVATO

MANDATO EJUS AC SUMPTIBUS LARGE EFFUSIS

EXSCRIPTUM,

INDIA DENIQUE TYPIS MANDATUM,

GRATI MONIMENTUM ANIMI

SUMMA QUA PAR EST OBSERVANTIA

DICANT

EDITORES DEVINCTISSIMI.

Widmung an den nicht genannten Mäzen [Kingsborough]

6
3. White Hall Place
December 13th 1831

Sir,
I hasten to thank you for your last letter dated Paris Nov. 21st, enclosing to me Mr. Remusats letter, and the estimate of what might be the cost of copying the Mexican Paintings preserved in the royal Library at Paris, together with a specimen of a page of the larger MS – Although normally unwilling to trespass too much upon your politesse, I am going to request the further favour of you obliging me by immediately engaging two artists (many of whom competent for the execution of any task can in a moment be found in Paris) to take tracings in facsimile of the shorter of those paintings, that is to say, of the one entitled alaja preciosa[33] consisting of 56 small pages [/]

---

33   Älterer Sprachgebrauch für *alhaja preciosa* – kostbares Juwel.

forming about 26 pages in folio – of that which professes to be a report to Montezuma from his spies, and the genealogical table in six pages. My reason for wishing two artists to be employed is, that being obliged to leave London in three weeks for Ireland, I am anxious to obtain copies of three paintings before my departure, and having had already experience of the short span of time in which the most intricate Mexican paintings can be copied, I rely upon your kind exertions to have copies of these paintings sent me to London within that span of time. Being occupied at the present moment in the composition of the eighth volume of the work, of which I shall hope in two or three months to have the pleasure of presenting you with a copy, I am anxious to have the opportunity of inspecting these paintings which may throw light on some of my enquiries – I had written so far when I received your last letter dated Paris Dec. 5th from which I perceive that you have not, although you certainly ought long since to have received a large box left at the residence of the Prussian Ambassador by Mr. Hering and directed to you, which contains 7 vols. of the Antiquities of Mexico[34], and two copies of the Grammar of Premare, one of which I beg you will inform Baron de Humboldt with every expression of my respect that I request his acceptance of – I should apologize to you for the great haste in which I have written this letter, and its consequent illy ability but I am unwilling to lose this evenings post, and hope you will be able to decypher it.
I have the honor to remain Sir
Your very Obedient Humble Servt
Kingsborough

7
3. White Hall Place
December 22d 1831

Sir,
I have just had the pleasure of receiving your letter dated Paris Dec. 20th. I request you to inform Mr. Remusat that I am obliged to him for his offer to accommodate the artist I may employ in his apartments, and Mr. Modin? can immediately commence the work on the terms proposed by Mr. Levasseur[35]. I should not however for the sake of lessening the expense wish the heads of any other figures to be omitted, as I wish the copies to be a perfect facsimile of the originals. I leave London on Monday next for Ireland and therefore consider myself fortunate in having already heard from you. Your acquaintance with Oriental literature and the possibility of your some day bestowing attention on the many dialects of the American continent makes me take this opportunity of stressing that I have a great many grammars of American languages published and in MS, which should you wish to inspect these, would at any time be very much? at your service, as I would have these sent for to Mitchelstown my fathers residence in Ireland on purpose. You mentioned to me in a former letter that you contemplated a work the object of which would be to point out the analogies between Hebrew and certain dialects of Asia and this is the reason of my mentioning these grammars the number of which will partially be soon much increased.

---

34 Band 8 und 9 des Werkes erschienen posthum.
35 J. C. V. Levasseur, Vermessungsingenieur, Mitglied der Société asiatique, der 1829 den chinesischen Text des Romans *Yujiaoli* herausgab.

I have the honor to remain Sir
Your most Obdt. Humble Servt.
Kingsborough

I have forgotten to observe that the value of the Le Terrier? MS is much enhanced by the names being added to the hieroglyphics as with the explanations in Spanish. I hope the transcriber will be very accurate in []36

8

Mitchelstown Castle, Ansicht aus John Preston Neale: *Views of the seats of noblemen and gentlemen, in England, Wales, Scotland and Ireland.* (London 1819–1823)

Mitchelstown Castle
January 28th 1832

Sir
In the last letter which you did me the honour of addressing to me of the date of December the 30th you informed me that you hoped soon to be able to transmit to me the copies of the Mexican Paintings which I wished first to have, together with a copy of your memoir on the origin of the different kinds of writing employed in the early ages of the world. As I feel very anxious about the safe arrival of a parcel which will contain such interesting documents, may I beg this favour of you having it enclosed in a desk [?] box, and sent to 3 White Hall Place, from whence it will be transmitted by the safest envoyance to me at Mitchelstown and with as little delay as possible. I beg Sir, that you will excuse the trouble? which I fear I am occasioning you

---

36   Textverlust.

and remain with every sentiment of respect
Your Obedt. Humble Servant
Kingsborough

9
Mitchelstown
March 24 1832

Sir

I am happy to learn from your letter dated March 5th that you have received the parcel containing the books. Allow me to return you my best thanks for dispatching to me the parcels containing the Mexican Paintings which I expect soon to receive as I am informed it has arrived in Cork.
I have the honour to remain
Your Obdt. Servt.
Kingsborough

10
Mitchelstown Castle
July 11th 1832

Sir

I feel myself under great obligation to you for the trouble which you have so kindly taken to forward my views at the Royal Library at Paris. I shall wish without delay to my bankers in London to remit you the sum of 2000 franks which payment in advance will perhaps encourage the artist to proceed rapidly with his task. The remainder of the sum which I agreed to give him shall be paid on its completion.

The leaf which you enclosed me is not in the least injured, and I can judge of the accuracy of the artist from having seen the [/] original painting of which it forms a page, and which I believe must have been brought from the coast of Yucatan, since its style is evidently not Mexican. I did not judge it worthy of a place in my collection of Mexican paintings on account of the figures being so much defaced in consequence of the decay of the plaster upon the leaves but the Dresden painting affords a sufficient specimen of the characters and symbols it contains so analogous to those discussed by M. Dupaix[37] in the temple of Palenque. I must here observe that it was not my original intention to include in that collection every rude fragment of Mexican paintings that may have escaped the ravages of time, but only such paintings as were preserved in the Bodleian Library at Oxford and the celebrated libraries of Europe, the authenticity of which could not be doubted, and the preservation of which was perfect. On this [/] principle I have excluded a great many fragments of paintings which were sent me from Mexico which had no

---

[37] Guillermo Dupaix (1746–1817), ein in Luxemburg geborener Österreicher flämischer Nationalität, der 1790 nach Mexiko ging, im Militär diente, dem es aber gelang, die Real Expedición Anticuaria zur Aufnahme der dortigen Altertümer zu organisieren und 1805–1809 in gemeinsamer Arbeit mit dem Zeichner José Castañeda wertvolles Material zusammentrug. Hatte ein getreuer Nachlaßverwalter für die Fertigstellung der Berichte und die Sicherstellung der Sammlungen gesorgt, so änderte sich das mit Mexikos Unabhängigkeit. der Nachlaßverwalter ging nach Spanien, eine Infrastruktur mußte in Mexiko erst aufgebaut werden und so gelang es dem jungen Latour Allard 1824 die Sammlung zu erwerben. Vgl. Marie-France Fauvet-Berthelot, Leonardo López Luján, Susana Guimarâes: The Real Expedición Anticuaria Collection. *Fanning the sacred flame. Mesoamerican studies in honor of H. B. Nicholson.* Boulder, CO: Univ. Pr. of Colorado 2012, Kap. 19.

relation to antiquities and could not be supposed to have been drawn by the ancient Mexicans, and shall exclude the paintings already copied in the Royal Library at Paris, which with the exception of the first do not possess the least real interest, even those paintings which are preserved in the Royal Library at Berlin and indebted to illustrious names, I mean of the Baron de Humboldt who brought them from Mexico, for the plan which […] occupy in these Volumes, as I […][38] not consider them very interesting. The only Mexican MS now existing in the Royal Library at Paris, of which I am very anxious to possess a copy is the Terier[39], which I intend should form an appendix to my work, as to the numerous phonetic symbols which it contains, will serve to illustrate a most interesting MS now in progress of printing for which I am indebted to the generosity of a Sovereign. Might I request that you would have the goodness to employ some competent Spaniard many of them I am informed are now resident in Paris, to copy. The text which accompanies the Terier MS^t which I do not doubt with fervour? is highly interesting.
I have the honor to remain Sir with sentiments of esteem
Your Obt. Humble Servant
Kingsborough

11

Mitchelstown
August 6th 1832

Sir
I feel extremely obliged to your letter dated Paris, July the 30th, in which you inform me that it is your intention to inscribe your work on the hieroglyphical discoveries of M. Champollion to me. Were I much less attached to literary and scientific pursuits than I am, I still should feel very sensible of the honour you intend me. I have to regret that the packet containing your Essay sur les écritures and doubtless the letter also to which you allude, has not yet reached me, but I shall lose no time in writing to White Hall Place to desire that it should be immediately forwarded to me. As I presume that you have by this time had leisure to cast your eyes over the contents of the sixth volume of the Antiquities of Mexico, the entire of which volume both translations and notes, has been written by me with the design of illustrating the resemblance of the Mexican form of government to the ancient Jewish theocracy, I should be extremely glad to know whether it is in your opinion that the agreements which I have used give at least a strong degree of probability to my theory. I reserve for another volume what I consider demonstrative proofs of that which I am content the reader the reader of the sixth volume should deem at present probability. I hope that this by time you will have heard from my banker and thanking you for all the trouble which you have taken about the facsimiles of the Mexican Paintings
I have the honour to remain Sir
with sentiments of regard
Your Obedt. Humble Servant
Kingsborough

---

38   Geringer Textverlust.
39   Gemeint ist wohl der Codex Telleriano-Remensis, benannt nach Charles Maurice Le Tellier, Erzbischof von Reims.

12

Paris, 1 Sept. 34

my Lord, I have the honour of transmitting to you the inclosed letter from the Secretary of the Institute of France acknowledging the receipt of the copy of your magnificent work which, according to the wishes of mr. Rich[40], I presented to the academie des Sciences in the sitting of the 24th of august last. a commission of several members has been appointed for the purpose of giving an account of this treasure.

I have informed mr. Rich of several documents concerning mexican antiquities lately brought to Paris of which he might procure copies on his return to this City. – mr. Baradère[41] is here preparing for publication the original mss. and drawings, which he lately brought from Mexico and concerning Palenqué. about two years since I made a Report on those antiquities to the antiquarian and geographical societies of Paris, awaiting myself of the collection of mr. Latour Allard[42] which form a part of your work. I pray (?), my Lord, to accept the assurance of my great respect D. B. Warden[43]

Rue du Pot de Fer St. Sulpice, no. 12

The Right Honble Lord Kingsborough, London, Whitehall Place, no. 3.

Schriftprobe Kingsboroughs

---

40   Obadiah Rich, 1777–1850, amerikanischer Diplomat, Büchersammler und Bibliograph.

41   Wohl der Abt Jean Henri Baradère, der 1834 in Paris die *Antiquités mexicaines* (Paris: Didot) herausgab.

42   Latour Allard (1799–), aus einer französischstämmigen Familie in New Orleans, reiste 1824 in Mexiko, wo er die Dupaix-Sammlung (s.o.) erwarb und nach Frankreich nahm, wo er sie allerdings nur unter Schwierigkeiten verkaufen konnte. Heute befindet sie sich im Musée Quai Branly in Paris.

43   David Bailie Warden, 1772–1845 Paris, Diplomat, Büchersammler, Schriftsteller, Mitglied der Société de Géographie. Er gab 1829 einen Rapport de la commission de La Société royale des Antiquaires de France. *Bulletin de la Société de Géographie* 12.1829, 43–48

Ein vergessener Gelehrter
William Huttmann (9. März 1792 – 3. Okt. 1844) und seine Briefe an Julius Klaproth

Übersicht

Zu den wenigen, die sich Anfang des 19. Jahrhunderts mit der chinesischen und mandschurischen Sprache befaßten und die weitgehend unbekannt geblieben sind, gehört William Huttmann. Außer einigen Veröffentlichungen, von denen seine Abhandlung über chinesische Landkarten gelegentlich genannt wird, waren kaum Spuren zu finden, die er hinterlassen hat. Die beiden Gesellschaften, mit denen er verbunden war, besitzen kein Material über ihn, und so bleibt als wichtigste Quelle der Nachruf im *Asiatic Journal* (AJ). Die beiden weiteren, kürzeren Würdigungen decken sich im Wesentlichen mit dem AJ. Von einem Nachlaß ist nichts bekannt geworden. Auch sind kaum Briefe von ihm nachzuweisen; eine Ausnahme sind seine zahlreichen Briefe an Julius Klaproth, die im Petersburger Akademie-Archiv erhalten sind und die nachstehend erstmals veröffentlicht werden. Nach Mendes Hinweis[44] schien Huttmanns Korrespondenz im Archiv der British & Foreign Bible Society in Cambridge vorhanden zu sein, was sich jedoch nicht bestätigte (Auskunft vom 9. Dez. 2020).

Biographisches

Mr. William Huttmann. – The death of this very able Chinese scholar, and the consequent loss of the stores of philological knowledge which he had accumulated during thirty years' application to the Chinese, Japanese, Mandchoo, and Mongolian languages, may be regarded as a public calamity. His history affords an example of the success with which patient industry and perseverance may oppose adverse circumstances.

Mr. Huttmann was born in London on the 9th March, 1792. He was destined to be a missionary, and this was the original cause of his studying the language of China, intended to be the scene of his labours. So successful was his application to this difficult tongue (for which at that time there were very few helps, Dr. Morrison's dictionary being yet unpublished), that, with the assistance of a native, at the early age of twenty-two, he could translate from it into English. The death of his father, in straightened circumstances, induced him to relinquish his intention of entering upon the career of a missionary, and, with a very commendable feeling, to employ his energies in contributing to the support of the younger branches of his family. He gradually extended his knowledge of languages till it embraced the following: – Chinese, Japanese, Mandchoo, Mongolian, Sanskrit, Bengali, Hindustani, Greek, Latin, German, French, Italian, and Dutch. With the first

---

44 Erling von Mende: Einige Bemerkungen zu den Druckausgaben des mandjurischen Neuen Testaments. *Oriens Extremus* 1972, 215–221, hier S. 217.

three of these tongues he was especially familiar; and during the time he was acquiring them and reading Chinese and Japanese works, he was struggling with narrow means, and emerging from those encumbrances under which the progress of merit is proverbially slow. He found time, however, for writing, and in 1820 he was instrumental in bringing out the *Annals of Oriental Literature*, the repository of many valuable papers, several of which were contributed by him, particularly a curious account of the Chinese army. When the *Asiatic Journal* commenced, he became a contributor to it; and amongst other articles furnished by him in its early numbers is one on the cultivation of tea, which was found useful in the experiments made to introduce the plant into the British territories in India. About the year 1828, his acquirements in Oriental philology recommended him to the Royal Asiatic Society, which appointed him assistant secretary; and on the formation of the Oriental Translation Fund, he was nominated its secretary. He retained both these situations till 1830 or 1831. About this time, unhappily, he became connected, as a part proprietor, with a newspaper called the *World*, which was the organ of a class of dissenters to which Mr. Huttmann himself (we believe) belonged, called the Congregational Dissenters, and shortly after he became its sole proprietor and editor. The speculation absorbed not only his time but his money, and plunged him into pecuniary embarassments, from which he never entirely extracted himself. Amongst its evil consequences was the dissolution of his connection with the Royal Asiatic Society.

Mr. Huttmann had now to recommence life, at the age of forty, with a young family. His skill as an Oriental linguist, which was great, and his acquirements in Chinese and Japanese literature, which were extensive, unfortunately yielded him few pecuniary resources: he gave instruction in these tongues, and he was employed occasionally by the East-India Company and by missionary institutions in the translation of documents. He still continued his contributions to periodical works; and he may, perhaps, claim the merit of having, in a letter published in the *Literary Gazette*, made suggestions which led to the institution of the Royal Geographic Society. During the latter months of his life he was employed in translating the New Testament into Chinese for the British and Foreign Bible Society.

Mr. Huttmann was twice married; he lost his second wife but a few months ago. He has left seven children, three of whom, under eight years of age, without father or mother, are totally improvided for. He died on the 5th October, of inflammation of the lungs, occasioned by a severe cold.

Huttmann war im Kreise der China-Interessierten durchaus anerkannt. So sprach der Lexikograph Antonio Montucci von „seinem gelehrten Freund" (*AJ* 16.1823: Montucci: My learned friend W. H. ...). Auch scheint der kritische Julius Klaproth (s.u.) ihn geschätzt zu haben, da für ihn Huttmann ein hilfsbereiter Agent und Resident in London war.

Erstaunlich ist es, daß Huttmann eine Übersetzung des *Chunqiu* 春秋, der Annalen des Fürstentums Lu, anzufertigen sich bereit erklärte (*AJ* 2.1830, 244: Mr. Huttmann, the secretary to the committee, also has offered to translate the Chun tsew of Confucius from the Chinese. This work, which still remains untranslated, contains the history of the kingdom of Loo, of which Confucius was some time prime minister, and is the only one of the works usually attributed to him which he really wrote.) Offenbar fand sich kein Mäzen, der bereit war, eine solche Arbeit zu finanzieren, worauf Huttmann angewiesen gewesen wäre.

Der Bruch in Huttmanns Laufbahn wird im Nachruf nur höflich angedeutet. Eine Mitteilung im *AJ* gibt die Erläuterung (Proceedings in *AJ* 8.1832, 231): The Council has now to discharge the painful task of reporting a serious dereliction of duty on the part of Mr. William Huttmann, one of its salaried officers, who, it regrets to state, had embezzled the sum of £107. 6 sh. 5 d. ....

Huttmanns Veröffentlichungen

Extracts from Chinese writers relating to the period when their characters were invented. By William Huttmann.
AJ 4.1817, 10–11

The life of Jesus Christ including his apocryphal history. From the spurious gospels, unpublished manuscripts, &c. &c. embellished with a head of Jesus. London: Sherwood, Neely, and Jones, W. Reynolds, Smith & Elder, 1818. VIII, 201 S.

A brief account of the origin and increase of the Chinese Tartarian army. By William Huttmann.
Annals of Oriental Literature 1–3.1820, 152–158

Notice and specimen of a Manchu Chinese dictionary. By William Huttmann.
Annals of Oriental Literature 1–3.1820, 553–557
Zit. Du Halde IV, 65–66 nach Parrenin
About three years since I was favored with the inspection of a printed specimen of a classed Mandchu, Mongol, and Chinese dictionary, with a Russian and Latin interpretation but unless it is very greatly improved of very little advantage to the public. The printed specimen was accompanied by one in MS. superior to it in every particular. Es handelt sich dabei um das Petersburger fünfsprachige Lexikonprojekt von Pavel Kamenskij, zu dem mehrere Gutachten angefordert wurden.

A notice of several Chinese-European dictionaries which have preceded Dr. Morrison's. (By William Huttmann.)
AJ 9.1821, 240–244

A notice of Dr. Morrison's Chinese dictionary. By Mr. Huttmann.
AJ 12.1821, 566–574

Chinese and Malay magazines. To the editor of the Asiatic Journal.
[Rez.] Malay Magazine. No. 2.1821. Published in Malayan, quarterly, at Malacca.
AJ 14.1822, 218–219
Wm. Huttmann

Countries favourable to the growth of tea. By William Huttmann.
AJ 14.1822, 556–560

Report of the proceedings of the first general meeting of the subscribers to the Oriental Translation Fund, with the prospectus, report of the committee, and regulations by William Huttmann; John Lewis Cox; Oriental Translation Fund. 1829. 16 S.

Report of the proceedings of the second general meeting of the subscribers to the Oriental Translation Fund, with the prospectus, report of the committee, and regulations.
1829. 31 S.
Die Reports liegen online auf.

The Manchu mode of expressing the sound of Chinese characters. To the editor
AJ 23.1837, 280–281
signed: 51, Burton Street, July 19th, 1837. William Huttmann

On the copper and paper money of China, by William Huttmann
The colonial magazine and commercial-maritime journal Vol. 2.1843, no. 9, pp. 409–417

On Chinese and European Maps of China / Huttmann, William.
Journal of the Royal Geographical Society of London, 14.1844, 117–127

William Huttmann [9.3.1792–3.10.1844]
AJ Nov. 1844, 104–105

The late William Huttmann.
The colonial magazine and commercial-maritime journal Vol. 3.[?]1844, 693

The late William Huttmann.
Fisher's colonial magazine and journal of trade, commerce and banking. Vol. 1 No. 11 (November 1844), 45

Ines von Racknitz: Mapmakers in China and Europe 1800–1844: The Perspective of *William Huttmann,* Royal Geographical Society. In: *Mapping Asia: Cartographic Encounters Between East and West.* Cham: Springer 2019, 233–246

The Sze shu or four books of Confucius: with a commentary & notes: (vol. 3, containing the second part of the Lun Yu, is wanting!) by Confucius; Mencius; William Marsden; W. Huttmann; / [S.l.: s.n., 18th cent?]
Exemplar in der King's College Library, London [nicht gesehen]

Zwei Briefe Huttmanns

Royal Asiatic Society House
Grafton Street London
May 11 1827

Sir

Being desirous of obtaining some Mandchu Mongol Calmuc and Japanese books and coins and knowing that you are acquainted with those languages I presume to request that you will oblige me by enquiring if such books or coins are purchasable in Russia – Should any of them be obtainable I would wither remit the money for them to Russia or pay any Russia merchant in London as the Bookseller might prefer.

Should you at any time have any literary Commissions for England I should feel a real pleasure in having their execution entrusted to me – I have the honor to be
Sir
With great respect
Your very obedient Servt.
Wm. Huttmann

Baron Schilling
St. Petersburg

St. Petersburg, Institut für Orientalische Handschriften, Russische Akademie der Wissenschaften, Orientalistenarchiv, Slg. Schilling von Canstadt (f. 56, op. 2, Nr 68)

Royal Asiatic Society House
Grafton Street London
July 17. 1827

Sir
I have the honor of transmitting to you the annexed resolution of the Committee of Correspondence of the Royal Asiatic Society.
I very much regret that your letters having been delayed nearly a month on the way to London and the adjourment (!) of the Committee of Correspondence from June to this day has prevented my replying sooner to your letter.
Hoping that you are enjoying health and prosperity, I remain
Sir
With sincere respect
Your Obedient Servant
Wm. Huttmann

The Rev. Professor Kidd[45]
Aberdeen

(Quelle: https://www.historicalautographs.co.uk/autographs/huttmann-william-17205/)

Eine wichtige Anregung, die tatsächlich aufgegriffen wurde, gab Huttmann durch einen Leserbrief in der *Literary Gazette* 1828: den Vorschlag zur Gründung einer Geographischen Gesellschaft:

---

[45] Man könnte denken an: Samuel Kidd (Welton 22. Nov. 1804–12. Juni 1843 Camden Town), Prof. am Anglo-Chinese College, Malacca (1824–1832); 1837–1842 Prof. des Chinesischen am University College London. – Aber Samuel Kidd war zu dieser Zeit in Malacca. So handelt es sich wohl um James Kidd DD (6. Nov. 1761–25. Dez. 1834), der 1793 zum Professor of Oriental Language (= Hebräisch) am Marischal College, Aberdeen ernannt wurde. http://www.openspacetrust.org.uk/?p=918

Geographical Society Proposed.

To the Editor of the Literary Gazette.

Sir, – After your favourable mention, in the *Literary Gazette* of the 24th of May, of the hint relating to the establishment of a Geographical Society, I confidently expected that some of your correspondents would immediately discuss the formation of such an institution.

My expectation having, however, been disappointed, and fearing that the answer to your correspondent may have escaped the notice of those who feel desirous of promoting geographical knowledge, I request you will spare me a small portion of your columns to direct or recall attention to this important subject.

No country is so deeply interested as England in the acquisition of a correct knowledge of the physical, moral, and political geography of every part of the world; yet, while we have societies for the cultivation of almost every other branch of knowledge, we have none for the cultivation of that science n which our political and commercial prosperity so greatly depends.

The non-existence of a Geographical Society in England cannot, I am certain, be traced to the want of proper persons to constitute it: for no nation abound so much as this country in voyagers and travellers; and the reading public generally considers the study of geography not less agreeable than instructive. Neither can its absence arise from the want of means for effectively executing the purposes for which such a society should be instituted; for we have active and intelligent fellow-countrymen either constantly visiting or residing in almost every part of the habitable globe.

As we enjoy the benefit and pleasure derived from geography, and are better circumstanced in reference to its cultivation than any other European nation – it may be inquired, why a Geographical Society has not long since been established in England? It is simply because no person possessing influence and energy has proposed its establishment. If the formation of a Geographical Society was proposed or zealously patronised by a few distinguished individuals, there is no doubt that a society, which would united the suffrages of the politician, the man of letters, and the merchant – would rapidly become eminent for its numbers and its utility.

It would be easy to enumerate the objects to which a Geographical Society should direct its attention, and the means by which they might be attained; but I will limit myself to stating, that I think statistics, the topography of the British Empire, and history so far as it is intimately connected with geography, should be included among its objects; and that furnishing travellers with topics of inquiry connected with the countries they visit, and encouraging them by conferring honorary distinctions, or pecuniary awards, and by the publication of their observations, – should be employed as means of increasing our geographical knowledge.

In conclusion, I take the liberty of stating my conviction of the strong probability, that geography, through being honoured and patronised, would be more generally and deeply studied, and thereby attain the rank of a science which it should, but does not at present, possess in England. I am yours, &c. W.H.

(Quelle: *Literary Gazette* 1828, S. 600.)

Notice and Specimen of a Mandchu Chinese Dictionary

This Dictionary, entitled Mandchu gisun ni buleku bitkhe [Manju gisun-i buleku bithe] in Mandchu, and Tsing ouen Kien (清文鑒 5065-3783-11604) in Chinese, is described generally by Parennin in Du Halde's *Histoire generale de la Chine*, tom. iv. 65,66.[46] Edition in folio.

„Sous le premier empereur Chun tchi 順治, qui ne régna que dix-sept ans, on commença à traduire les livres classiques de la Chine, et à faire des dictionnaires de mots, rangez selon l'ordre alphabétique; mais comme les explications et les caractères étoient en chinois, et que la langue Chinoise ne pouvoit rendre ni les sons ni les mots de la langue Tartare, ce travail fut assez inutile.

C'est pour cette raison que l'empereur Cang hi 康熙, dès le commencement de son règne, érigea un tribunal de tout ce qu'il y avoit à Peking de plus habiles gens dans les deux langues Tartare et Chinoise; it fit travailler les uns à la version de l'histoire et des livres classiques qui n'étoient pas achevés; les autres, aux traductions des pièces d'éloquence; et le plus grande nombre, à composer un Trésor de la langue Tartare.

Cet ouvrage s'exécuta avec une diligence extraordinaire. S'il survenoit quelque doute, on interrogeoit les vieillards des huit banières Tartares; et s'il étoit nécessaire d'une plus grande recherche, on consultoit ceux qui arrivoient nouvellement du fond de leur pays. On proposoit des récompenses à ceux qui déterreroient quelques vieux mots, quelques anciennes expressions propres à être placées dans le Trésor. On affectoit ensuite de s'en servir pour les aprendre à ceux qui les avoient oubliées, ou plutôt qui n'en avoient jamais eu connoissance.

Lorsque tous ces mots furent rassemblez, et qu'on crût qu'il n'y en manquoit que très-peu qui pouroient se mettre dans un suplément, on les distribua par classes.

La première classe parle du ciel; la seconde, du tems; la troisième, de la terre; la quatrième, de l'empereur, du gouvernement des mandarins, des cérémonies, des coutumes, de la musique, des livres, de la guerre, de la chasse, de l'homme, des terres, des soyes, des toiles, des habits, des instrumens, du travail, des ouvriers, des barques, du boire, du manger, des grains, des herbes, des oiseaux, des animaux domestiques & sauvages, des poissons, des vers, &c.

Chacune de ces classes est divisée en chapitres & en articles. Tous les mots ainsi rangez et écrits en lettres majuscules, on met sous chacun, en plus petits caractères, la définition, l'explication et l'usage du mot. Les explications sont nettes, élégantes, d'un style aisé; et c'est en les imitant qu'on aprend à bien écrire.

Comme ce livre est écrit en langue & en caractères Tartares, il n'est d'aucune utilité pour les commençans, et ne peut servir qu'à ceux qui, sçachant dejà la langue, veulent s'y perfectionner, ou composer quelque ouvrage."

The arrangement of the words in classes is not peculiar to this Dictionary, the same arrangement is found in the Chinese Dictionary Hay pien (海篇 4993-7538)[47] and in the Chinese and Japanese Encyclopedias.[48]

---

46 Hier geprüft an der Ausgabe Henri Scheurleer 1736, wo sich der Text S.77–78 befindet. Der Titel, hier verwechselt mit dem großen Werk des P. Moyriac de Mailla, lautet natürlich: *Description géographique, historique, chronologique, politique et physique de l'empire de la Chine.*

47 *Fundgruben des Orients*, Band 4, 183–201: Fan, Sifan, Man, Meng, Han tsi yao, our recueil nécessaire des mots sanskrits, tangutains, mandchous, mongols et chinois.

48 See Fourmont's Meditationes Sinicae, 124–125.

M. Remusat[49] has translated part of a Sanskrit, Tibetan, Manchu, Mongol and Chinese Vocabulary, arranged on a nearly similar plan, and the words in several Sanskrit Dictionaries are classed according to subjects; but whether the Chinese adopted the Hindu system, or invented one for themselves, I am unable to determine.

Part of the first preface is printed with Mandchu type in the 8vo edition of Langlès' Alphabet Mantchou, 63–66, and a translation, 67–69, of which some of the errors are corrected in Klaproth's Grande Exécution d'Automne, 4–6, and 45, 46. There is a second preface in Mandchu and Chinese, of which the Mandchu is printed by M. Langles, with a French translation, 76–89.

A table of all the words, arranged according to the principles of the Mandchu Syllabarium, is placed at the head of the Dictionary, with references to the articles in which they occur. The pronunciation of the Mandchu words is expressed in Chinese by giving the initial and final characters of each syllable, as to express the word enduri (a spirit) they write, e-en-En (12241-2839) tu u, du (12240-5421) li-i, ri (1252-130). The pronunciation of the Chinese characters is given in Mandchu letters. I have followed the Mandchu pronunciation in the accompanying specimen, in preference to that of the De Guignes' Dictionary, to which the figures refer:

Specimen of the Mandchu Chinese Dictionary

Enduri i khatsin – Chen lui [shenlei] 神類 (7025-12251) Chapter of beneficent spirits.

Abkai khan. Cheng ti [Shangdi] 上帝 (7-2421) – The supreme King of heaven is called Abkai khan, the Emperor of heaven.

Enduri – Chen [shen] 神 (7025). The animating principle is called Enduri, the spirit. All invisible and inaudible beings, to whose honour images are placed in temples, and sacrifices offered, are called Enduri, spirits.

Wetcheku – Chen Ki [Shenzhi] 神祇 (7025-7018) The Spirit to whom sacrifices are offered in the house is called Wetcheku [wejeku] – The Spirit of the earth.

Soko. The Chinese name is the same as the above; synonimous [!] with Wetcheku, as is also Wetcheku Soko.

Amba boikhon enduri. Tai che [Taishe] 太社 (1799-6994) The Spirit who presides in chief over terrestrial affairs is called Amba boikhon enduri – The great Spirit of the earth.

Amba dcheku enduri. Tai tsi 太稷 (1799-7212) The Spirit who presides in chief over the productions of the earth is called Amba dcheku enduri – The great grain Spirit.

Abkai bantsibunga enduri – Tian heu chen 天后神 (1798-1143-7025). When Yang and Yng, the active and passive principles had generated the empyreum, the Spirit which assumed its government was called Abkai bandsibunga enduri – The Spirit who is queen of heaven.

Omosi mama Fu chen [Fushen] 福神 (7063–7025) The Spirit to whom those sacrifice who desire happiness is called Omosi mama, the Spirit of happiness.

Sure mama – Teu tchen chen [Douzhen shen] 痘疹神 (6331-6297-7025) The Spirit invoked in favour of children who have the small-pox is called Sure mama, the Spirit of the small-pox.

---

49   See in Remusat's memoire sur les livres Chinois de la bibliothèque du Roi, 12–14, a notice of the louy chu san tsay tou hoey [leishu sancai tuhui 類書三才圖會] (12257-4019-6-3226-1543-4025).

Wali mama – Wa li ma ma 瓦立媽媽 (6083-7355-1994-1994) There is a piece of cloth, hung by a thread behind the door, to which all manufactured and raw articles that are brought into the houses are shewn – This hanging cloth is called Wali mama.

The above specimen fills two pages in the Dictionary, the chapter of spirits contains two pages more in the body of the work, and 12 in the Supplement.

The whole of the Dictionary, consisting of 52 thin 8vo volumes has been translated into Mongolian, and printed at Peking, in 20 thick 8vo volumes, in the year 1717. M. Klaproth has a MS. Russian translation of the two first of these volumes[50], and a French or English translation of the whole would be of essential advantage to the student of the Chinese or Mandchu Tartar languages, as it contains a multitude of compound terms and illustrations which will not be found in either of the Chinese European Dictionaries now publishing.

An alphabetical Mandchu Dictionary was published at Peking in 1752, entitled Mandchu isabukha bitkhe [Manju isabuha bithe]. This Dictionary was translated by Pere Amiot, and published by M. Langlès, in three quarto volumes, at Paris, in the years 1789–90. M. Rémusat, who places the publication of the original in the year 1750, remarks, that „Le Dictionnaire Tartare Mandchou d'Amiot n'est assurément pas tel qu'il auroit été, si l'auteur eût prévu qu'on livreroit son travail à l'impression sans lui subir une rédaction préalable."[51] M. Klaproth, after noticing the existence of another alphabetical Dictionary more exact in its definitions, and containing many more ancient words than Amiots, observes, „Dans le Dictionnaire du P. Amiot, manque souvent la première et principale signification, et indépendamment des obscurités, M. Amiot a si mal traduit l'explication des mots Mandchou, que son ouvrage est presque inutile à tous ceux qui ne peuvent pas consulter l'original Chinois."[52] A MS. Mandchu Latin Dictionary in the Royal Society's Library greatly excels Amiots in copiousness and exactness; but has all the examples written in Latin letters only, and the whole, excepting the Mandchu letters, is very minutely, and, in some places, almost illegibly written.

About three years since I was favored with the inspection of a printed specimen of a classed Mandchu, Mongol, and Chinese Dictionary, with a Russian and Latin interpretation; but unless it is very greatly improved in passing trough the press, it will be of very little advantage to the public. The printed specimen was accompanied by one in MS. superior to it in every particular.[53]

Briefe an Julius Klaproth

Huttmanns orthographische Eigenheiten (z.B. Verwendung des sächsischen Genitivs ohne Apostroph, Auslassung des e im Präteritum, z.B. addressd, fehlende Satzzeichen sind beibehalten worden. Für die Satz- und Periodengliederung benutzte er gern Gedankenstriche.

---

50   Klaproth's *Sprache und Schrift der Uiguren*, 5.
51   *Recherches sur les langues Tartares*. tom. i 128.
52   *Grande exécution d'Automne*, No. ii. 10.
53   Es handelt sich dabei um das Wörterbuch der Russischen Mission, dessen Druck von P. Kamenskij betreut werden sollte. Da dieser indes als Leiter der Mission nach China abberufen wurde, kam das Projekt zum Stillstand, da in St. Petersburg niemand die Leitung übernehmen konnte. – Im Bestand *Schilling von Canstadt* im Orientalistenarchiv des Instituts für Orientalische Manuskripte der Russ. Akademie der Wissenschaften, St. Petersburg, befindet sich ein Konvolut mit Beurteilungen und Äußerungen zum Projekt; es wäre sicherlich der Edition wert. [Es ist inzwischen in Bearbeitung.]

Übersicht[54]

10	10. Jan. 1822	490	2. März 1829
11	10. Juni 1822	510	27. Mrz 1829
30	1. Nov. 1822	520	o.D.
	24. Aug. 1822 an Longman & Co.	530	1. April 1829
	31. Aug. 1833 an Kingsbury & Co.	550	10. April 1829
50	24. Aug. 1825	560	1. Juli 1829
70	6. Sept. 1825	570	16. Juli 1829
80	19. Sept. 1925	580	29. Aug. 1829
100	13. Dez. 1825	600	6. Okt. 1829
120	18. Jan. 1826	610	23. Nov. 1829
140	30. März 1826	630	1. Febr. 1830
160	18. Apr. 1826	640	17. Febr. 1830
180	11. Sept. 1826	660	15. März 1830
190	13. Nov. 1826	680	20. April 1830
210	26. Juli 1827	700	1. Mai 1830
220	o. D. von G. Th. Staunton	720	29. Mai 1830
230	31. Okt. 1827	740	18. Aug. 1830
240	29. Nov. 1827	750	10. Sept. 1830
260	28. Jan. 1828	760	1. Okt. 1830
280	2. Febr. 1828	770	19. Okt. 1830
290	2. Febr. 1828	790	1. Nov. 1830
300	29. Febr. 1828	810	30. Nov. 1830
320	1. Mai 1828	820	4. Dez. 1830
330	PS zum vorigen	840	5. Nov. 1830
340	1. Juli 1828	850	17. Dez. 1830
360	7. Juli 1828	870	21. Dez. 1830
370	1. Sept. 1828	880	o. D.
380	30. Sept. 1828	890	6. Jan. 1831
390	3. Okt. 1828	900	11. Jan. 1831
400	12. Nov. 1828	920	18. Jan. 1831
420	1. Dez. 1828	940	20. Mai 1831
430	16. Dez. 1828	950	7. Juni 1831
450	2. Febr. 1829	970	1. Okt. 1831
470	9. Febr. 1829		

10

Explanation of the Afghāni or Pashtu Alphabet according to the Grammar and Dictionary of the Naváb Muhabbat Khan, a MS. in the East India Company's Library

ا	ă
ب	b
پ	p
ت	t dental
ٹ	t pronounced from the roof of the mouth as the Nagari letter
ج	j as in the English word James
چ	ch as in the English words charity, Charles etc.
	directed to be pronounced something between ج & چ
خ	kh as in the Persian word
ژ	directed to be pronounced something between خ Persian and Nágari
د	d dental

---

d pronounced from the roof of the mouth as the Nagari letter and as in the Hindi
words dál and dhál a shield.

ر   r English

ر   r as in the Hindi words bhir or bhir

ز   z as in the Persian word زر zar or روز roz

ژ   as in the Persian word ژاله jálah hail, or in the French words jai

س   s English

ش   sh English, ch French

غ   as in the Arabic word غیرت ghairat

ق   k as in the Arabic word قریم kadim

ک   k as in the Persian words کار kár کنار kanár

گ   g as in the English word gun or the Persian guzar

ل   l

م   m

ن   n

ن   ng as in the English word king

و   occasionally as o, w, u and v

ه   h as in the words هوا hawa, شاة Shah, Mah etc.

ي   occasionally i, e, y

11

N. 2 Catharine Street Stepney
June 10th 1822

Sir

Annexed to this letter is an explanation of the Pushtoo Alphabet extracted from a Persian
MS by a Gentleman attached to the East India House – As no Pushtoo Grammar is printed,
I was obliged to defer answering your letter until I could obtain this explanation.

On enquiry at the Bible Society's Depot I was informed that they have sent 12 copies
of each of their translations to the Bible Society at Paris for sale etc. and that they have
no more for distribution. Should you however be unable to procure from the Parisian
Society all the translations you want on your writing to me I will endeavor to procure
those which are deficient.

I have also got from the Baptist Missionary Society a list of their translations priced.
This list I hope you have received along with Sir G. T. Stauntons Miscellaneous
Translations[55] (which he sent to me for transmission to you) and 2 or 3 other publications.

All the works printed Malacca and offered for sale in London have I believed been
already forwarded to you – and I lately sent you Dr. Milnes History of the Malacca
Mission[56] containing a lot of all the books printed there – Should you particularly wish to
acquire any of them I will write to my brother at Malacca who will if possible send me
copies – I hope soon to receive from him the 7th number of the [Indo-Chinese] Gleaner
for which I wrote above a year since.

---

55   *Miscellaneous notices relating to China, and our commercial intercourse with that country, including a few
      translations from the Chinese language.* By George Thomas Staunton ... London: J. Murray 1822. IX,432 S.

56   *A Retrospect of the first ten years of the Protestant mission to China:* (now, in connection with the Malay,
      denominated the ultra-Ganges missions) accompanied with miscellaneous remarks on the literature, history,
      and mythology of China &c. by William Milne. Malacca: Anglo-Chinese Press 1820. VIII, 376 S.

The 4th part of Morrisons Dictionary was laying in the East India Warehouse some months before it was purchaseable of Truettell [!] Würtz & Co. and hope it has been long since received.

I am extremely obliged by your favoring me with the Proofsheets of your Asiatic Memoirs. The life of Buddha and the article on the Asiatic historians are particularly valuable and interesting. As your works have been published in various places and under various circumstances even Oriental scholars are scarcely aware of their number and utility – If you therefore would favor me with a list of them I will endeavor to obtain its insertion in the Asiatic Journal to shew the lovers of oriental literature how extensively and successfully you have cultivated an acquaintance with the languages and literature of Asia. You would also oblige me by mentioning when it is likely the Second part of your Supplement to Basiles Dictionary[57] will be published.

Sir G. T. Staunton was the Gentleman to whom Dr. Montuccis reply to the Gleaner was submitted and the author of the letter printed in part in that article. I had no authority to correct errors when I was requested to procure its publication and cannot be considered responsible for its contents. Indeed I merely read the rough draft of the article some months before it was printed and have not read it at all in print –

Hoping to be of soon honored with another letter

I remain Sir Respectfully Your Obedient Servant

Wm Huttmann

30

2 Catharine Street Stepney

Nov. 1st 1822

Sir

I very much regret that I am not able to report the success of my endeavors to obtain a purchaser for your description of China & Tibet and of the MS route to Laddak.

You will annexed find the correspondence on the subject of your geographical works with the Houses Longman & Co. and Kingsbury & Co. – I did not apply to Murray in consequence of his not noticing an application I made to him formerly for one of the Parisian Literati and I was unwilling to have my letters treated with neglect a second time.

Supposing that the East India Company might wish to obtain the route to Laddak I extracted the part of your letter relating to it and accompanied by the plan of the route sent it to Dr. Wilkins[58] their Librarian and Literary Adviser but as he was informed by a Russian Nobleman that there are later surveys in Print which is I think rather doubtful the company declined availing themselves of an opportunity of adding to their collection of Maps what I think might prove extremely useful.

Hoping that I may more successfully execute the next commissions your honor me with

I remain, Sir

respectfully Your Obliged Servant

William Huttmann

---

57   Durch das Erscheinen von Morrisons Wörterbuch war das von Basile (1813) obsolet geworden, so auch das Supplement, und so nahm Klaproth von dem ursprünglich vorgesehenen weiteren Supplement Abstand.

58   Charles Wilkins (Frome 1749–13. Mai 1836 London), britischer Orientalist und Begründer der Sanskritstudien: Er übersetzte die Bhagavadgita und verfaßte eine Sanskritgrammatik. er war in London als Bibliothekar der East India Company tätig. Klaproth widmete ihm den 1. Band seiner *Mémoires relatifs à l'Asie.*

Copy of a letter to Messrs. Longman & Co.
Augt 24th 1822

Gentleman

Mr. Klaproth having collected materials for a description of China & Thibet has requested me to inform him if I think any London Bookseller would purchase the MS. for publication.

Knowing that you publish many oriental works I have taken the liberty of enclosing for your perusal his letter describing the nature of the collection.

Mr. Klaproth is well known in the Literary world as the author of travels in the Caucasus and Georgia – A supplement to M. de Guignes Chinese and French Dictionary and many other works and is by his great knowledge of the Chinese Language and his geographical & statistical studies better qualified for compiling a topography of China than any other person in Europe. –

Should you think of purchasing M. Ks MS you can either inform that Gentleman or communicate to me your ideas on the subject.

Requesting you to return the letter and specimens of Maps as soon as you can make it convenient.

I remain, Gentlemen […]

This letter was sent to Kingsbury & Co. Augt. 31 1822.

Paternoster S[…]
Augt. 25 […]

Dear Sir

Pray accept our best thanks for your […] polite attention in sending us Mr. Klaproth's letter […]

On considering the matter we are apprehensive […] the sale of the works in question would not repay the necessary expenses, consequently we beg leave to decline entering into the speculation.

Believe us, Dear Sir, Yrs. &
(signed) Longman & Co.

Messrs Kingsbury Parbury & Allen present their Compliments to Mr. Huttmann & other with return the papers relating to M. Klaproth's Manuscript, & altho it would not answer their purpose to publish the same yet they thank Mr. H. for his application.

7 Leadenhall St.
24th Oct. 1822
This letter altho dated Oct. 24th was not handed to me until the evening of the 29th Wm. H.

50
11 Cornwall Place Holloway
London Aug. 24 1825
Sir

I this morning despatched through the Messageries Royales Frazers Khorasan[59] (£2-10-6) and the Asiatic Journal for August (2/9) – which I hope you will receive along with this Letter. –

I have sent to all the principal dealers in Second Hand Books for Kirkpatricks Nepaul[60] but cannot obtain it. A New copy would cost you about £2-2-0. –

On Mess[rs] Devaux & Co. paying me £7-2-0 I handed them a detailed account which I supposed they would forward to you as I learn from your letter that they have not done so. I have written to request that they will send a copy of it to either you or me immediately.

When you have occasion to honor me with a letter I should be particularly obliged by your informing me when M. Remusats notice of the Japanese Encyclopedia[61] and the New edition of Rodrigues's Japanese Grammar[62] will be obtainable as I am very desirous of obtaining early copies of those works. Any letter for me may either be addresses to Holloway as above or to the Royal Asiatic Societys Houses as I have had the appointment of Assistant Secretary nearly 3 months.

An announcement of your Magazin Asiatique[63] will appear in the next number of the Asiatic Journal. – I shall anxiously wait for the appearance of the first number as its contents promise to be peculiarly interesting.

Could you oblige me with one of 和致 of the 元 dynasty coins if you have a duplicate? I would not presume to solicit this favor was it not to extricate a Gentleman from a difficulty – Mr. Marsden[64] is publishing a catalogue of his Oriental coins – in the text of the work he has referrd to Che ho [money durchgestrichen] of the Yuen dynasty money but has mislaid the coin so that he cannot have it engraved to correspond with the reference in the body of his book – If you should be able to let me have one perhaps you will be so good as to send it by Post as the Engraver is waiting for that coin.

I have been endeavoring to procure Collados Japanese Dictionary[65] for several years but have not succeeded if you would oblige me by ordering it of Messrs Dondey-Dupré

59   James Baillie Fraser: *Narrative of a journey into Khorasān in the years 1821 and 1822. including some account of the countries to the North-East of Persia*; with remarks upon the national character, government, and resources of that kingdom. London: Longman, Hurst, Rees, Ormem Brown, and Green 1825. XXVI S., [1] Bl., 623, [148] S.

60   William Kirkpatrick: *An account of the kingdom of Nepaul: being the substance of observations made during a mission to that country in the year 1793*, by colonel Kirkpatrick. London: Miller 1811. XIX, 386 S.

61   J. P. Abel-Rémusat: Notice sur l'Encyclopédie Japonaise et sur quelques ouvrages du même genre. *Notices et extraits des manuscrits de la Bibliothèque nationale*. 11.1827, 123–310.

62   *Élémens de la grammaire japonaise*, par le P. Rodriguez. Traduits du Portugais sur le manuscrit de la Bibliothèque du Roi, et soigneusement collationnés avec la grammaire publiée par le même auteur à Nagasaki en 1604, par M. Landresse. Précédés d'une explication des Syllabaires japonais, et de deux planches contenant les signes de ces syllabaires, par M. Abel-Rémusat. Paris: Dondey-Dupré 1825. XX, 142 S. Supplément. Paris 1826. 31 S.

63   *Magasin asiatique, ou Revue géographique et historique de l'Asie centrale et septentrionale*; publié par Mr. J. Klaproth, membre des Sociétés asiatiques de Paris et de Londres. Paris: Dondey-Dupré 1835 [vielm. 1825]. 329 S.

64   William Marsden (Verval 16. Nov. 1754–6. Okt. 1836), Orientalist, Mitarbeiter der East India Company, Erforscher Sumatras. Vgl. seinen Münzkatalog: *Numismata Orientalia Illustrata: The Oriental Coins, Ancient And Modern, Of His Collection, Described And Historically Illustrated* by William Marsden. F.R.S. &c., &c. With Numerous Plates, From Drawings Made Under His Inspection. Part I. [Part II.] London: Printed For The Author, By Cox And Baylis, Great Queen Street, Lincoln's-Inn-Fields; And Sold By Longman, Hurst, Rees, Orme, and Brown, Paternoster-Row; and Kingsbury, Parbury and Allen, Leadenhall-Street. MDCCCXXIII. [MDCCCXXV] 2 Bände: XIX, [5], 840 S. (durchgehend paginiert), LVII Tafeln. 4°.

65   Diego Collado: *Ars grammaticae iaponicae lingvae* in gratiam et adivtorivm eorum, qui praedicandi Euangelij causa ad Iaponiae Regnum se voluerint conferre composita, & sacrae de Propaganda Fide Congregationi dicata à Fr. Didaco Collado Ordinis Praedicatorum per aliquot annos in praedicto Regno Fidei Catholicae propagationis Ministro. Roma: Propaganda Fide 1632. 75 S.

& Co. they could probably obtain one for me and I will pay by person in London for it whom they may name.

Hoping that you will excuse my troubling you with these requests

I remain Sir

With great admiration and respect

Your Obliged Servant

Wm. Huttmann

M. Jules de Klaproth

Paris

70

11 Cornwall Place Holloway

September 6 1825

Sir

I am extremely obliged by your prompt attention to my request relating to 和致 coin. Although Sir G. T. Staunton furnished Mr. Marsden with the names of his coins yet it is not impossible that 和政 might be mistaken for Che ho especially if the coin was a little defaced –

I have transcribed the passages from M. Wilsons History of Cashmir[66] which relate to Nagardjunas period of excellence which appears to have been after Saeya Sinha

Hoping that you will never hesitate at commanding my sources when they can be usefully employed

I remain Sir

With great respect

Your Obedient Servant

Wm. Huttmann

M. Jules de Klaproth

à Paris

80

11 Cornwall Place Holloway

Sept. 19 1825

Sir

I very much regret that Thoms Chinese courtship[67] is not yet ready for publication and that a copy which was presented to me is lent – I expect however to have it returned on Thursday when I will forward it to you and replace it when the Book can be obtained at Kingsburys –

---

66 Horace Hayman Wilson: An essay of the Hindu history of Cashmir. *Asiatick researches* 15.1825, 1–119.
67 Peter Perring Thoms: *Chinese courtship; in verse;* to which is added, an appendix, treating of the revenue of China, &c. &c. London: Parbury, Allen, and Kingsbury 1824. XVI, 339 S.

I am extremely obliged by the Grammaire Japonaise also by your Histoire de Kachmir[68] + Widerlegung des Herrn Schmidt[69] copies of which I have forwarded to Mr. Colebrooke[70] and Mr. Marsden as directed.

I have written to Mr. Kirchner requesting permission to trouble him with a copy of the Asiatic Journal the last day of each month and doubt Not that he will forward one to you without delay. –

I remain Sir
Respectfully
Your obliged Servant
William Huttmann

M. Jules de Klaproth
à Paris

100
Grafton Street
December 13 1825

Sir

About a month since I had the pleasure of securing a copy of your Magazin Asiatique and immediately sent a note of its contents to the Editor of the Asiatic Journal who inserted it in the number for December – I have since at the editors request lent him the number so that he probably may give a more detailed notice of the interesting articles it furnishes.
In the parcel which I forward this day by the Messageries Royales is enclosed a Copy of the Malay Vocabulary and 2 or 3 Malayan tracts of which I request your acceptance –
Mr. Moreau the French Vice Consul who will write to you in a few days has requested me also to forward to you 2 copies of Statistical Tables relating to the East India Company and a Chinese Celestial Planisphere brought to London by Mr. Thoms who printed Dr. Morrisons Chinese Dictionary.

I have waited 2 or 3 days hoping to receive a parcel for you from Mr. Haughton[71] but will send it separately directly it arrives and pay whatever sum Mr. H. requires.

It gives me great pleasure to learn that the Second Volume of your Asiatic Memoirs is nearly ready for publication as that volume will I expect nearly or entirely complete my collection of pieces published by you in which there are at present several deficiencies – I very much regret that Rothschilds house has neglected sending you the Asiatic Journal – the number for November was delivered there on the 31st of October – that for December on the 30th of November. If you would indicate another channel for the conveyance it would probably reach you more regularly. –

---

68   Histoire de Kachmir, traduite de l'original sanskrit du Râdjâ Taringin'i, par M. H. Wilson; extraite et communiquée par M. Klaproth. *JA* 7,1825, 3–31, 65–90.

69   Klaproth: *Beleuchtung und Widerlegung der Forschungen über die Geschichte der mittelasiatischen Völker des Herrn J. J. Schmidt.* Paris: Dondey-Dupré 1924. 116 S.

70   Henry Thomas Colebrooke (London 15. Juni 1765– 10. März 1837 London), war im britischen Kolonialdienst in Indien tätig und wurde Professor für indisches Recht und Sanskrit. Er veröffentlichte eine Sanskritgrammatik (1805) und ein Sanskritwörtbuch (1808).

71   Graves Chamney Haughton (1788–1849), britischer Orientalist; er trat zunächst in die Dienste der East India Company, studierte in Calcutta und war von 1819 bis 1827 Professor für Sanskrit und Bengali am East India College in Haileybury. Er bewarb sich 1832 um die Boden Professur für Sanskrit, trat aber zugunsten von Wilson zurück. Vgl. Gordon Goodwin, J. B. Katz: Haughton, Graves Chamney (1788–1849). *Oxford Dictionary of National Biography* https://doi.org/10.1093/ref:odnb/12611.

Campbells Teloogoo Grammar[72] is not known to any of the London Booksellers – Westons conquest of the Meao Tse[73] is of very rare occurrence + Colebrookes Amara Cosha and Careys Mahratta Grammar[74] cannot be procured –

I was extremely gratified by learning from the Journal Asiatique that you have proposd [!] to the Société Asiatique the publication of a Japanese Dictionary – I know from personal experience that such a work is very much wanted as I have been for 7 years been endeavoring to obtain a Copy of Collados Dictionary and have not yet succeeded – Could I have obtained a Japanese Dictionary some years since I might now have been moderately proficient in the language instead of continuing in its elements.

The zeal and industry of your Asiatic Society is truly admirable and worthy of imitation and I should feel sincere pleasure in doing anything in my power to promote its interests. – I regret that I have nothing valuable to send as a donation but as I have duplicates of Dr. Morrisons English Grammar for Chinese and believe that there are very few copies in Europe I have enclosed one for the Societys Library and as Chinese coins are more easily procured in London than in Paris I have added a Set of those minted by the Ta tsing dynasty from Shun-tche to Taou-kwang.

In consequence of your Societys presenting our Asiatic Society with a Set of the Journal Asiatique and promising to forward copies of all its publications Dr. Noehden[75] countermanded the Journal Asiatique of the Bookseller who furnished our periodical publications – This countermand has occasiond much disappointment as your journal is frequently enquird for and our most recent number is the 33rd – Would it be possible for the Agent of your Society to furnish us with the deficient numbers and supply them in future? –

The account of Siam and Bombay Transactions are not likely to appear very soon.

Conformably with your request I subjoin a statement of your account no part of which has been paid by Messrs Devaux & Co. altho they express their willingness to pay it on the receipt of orders from you or Messrs Lelong & Co. – To prevent confusion - in future I will mark the prices of the Books on them with a black lead pencil.

Hoping that I shall soon have the pleasure of sending you Mr. Haughtons parcel.

I remain Sir

With great respect

Your Obedient Servant

Wm Huttmann

M. Jules de Klaproth

Paris

120

Holloway Jan. 18 1826

Sir

---

72 *A grammar of the Teloogoo language, commonly termed the Gentoo*, peculiar to the Hindoos inhabiting the North eastern provinces of the Indian peninsula by A. D. Campbell. Madras: College Press 1816. XXV, 208 S.

73 Stephen Weston: *The conquest of the Miao-Tse*. An imperial poem by Kien-lung. London 1810. 58 S., 6 Taf.

74 William Carey: *A grammar of the Mahratta language;* to which are added dialogues on familiar subjects. Serampore: Mission Press 1805. VIII, 152, 49 S.

75 Georg Heinrich Nöhden (Göttingen 23. Jan. 1780–14. März 1826 London), Kunsthistoriker, Aufseher am Britischen Museum, Sekretär der Asiatischen Gesellschaft in London, Verfasser einer deutschen Grammatik, Übersetzer von Dramen Schillers ins Englische.

Baron Maltzahn[76] very politely expressed his willingness to convey the Asiatic Journal to you Monthly – but as I expected to have got all the Books you ordered – that were obtainable – by the 2nd or 3rd Instant I supposd that you would receive it sooner if forwarded in your parcel than if conveyd through the Prussian Embassy – I perceive however that the parcel had not reachd you on the 11th but suppose that it must have reachd Paris directly after your letter was despatch'd. –

The Taheetian Books enclosd in the parcel were presented to me by the London Missionary Society. –

Mr Marsden knowing that I write to you occasionally sent me the enclosd Note a few days since which I take the liberty of enclosing for your perusal

On my applying to Mss^{rs} Longman & Co. on the subject of the Voyage à Peking they informd me that they had written to MM Dondey-Dupré offering £20 for the use of your Notes etc. They appear to consider your correction and additions extremely valuable and it is evident that there has scarcely ever been a Voyage publishd under such peculiar advantages as will attend your edition of Timkovski[77]. –

Messrs Devaux & Co. say that they have not yet receivd instructions from Messrs Lelong & Co or yourself to pay me £6.9.3 I therefore include that sum in the annexed statement.

I regret that Mr. Thoms[78] has not got the 2 other celestial charts necessary to complete a Chinese Atlas of the Heavens. – Neither has he any spare copies of the Map of Kwang tung nor of the English Grammar for Chinese – In the next parcel I have the pleasure of sending you I expect Mr. Thoms will enclose a copy of the Chinese courtship inscribd to you and one for M. Remusat.

The other Books you requested me to obtain are unfortunately not procurable at present but if you write for them on some future occasion copies may have come into the Booksellers hands –

Is it possible to obtain a copy of Collados Japanese Dictionary at Paris? I have applied to several foreign Booksellers in London for a copy but they have not been able to get one for me –

76   Bogislaw von Maltzahn (1793–1833), preußischer Gesandter in London.
77   Egor Timkovskij: *Voyage à Peking, à travers la Mongolie, en 1820 et 1821.* Ouvrage accompagné d'un atlas qui contient toutes les planches de l'original, et plusieurs autres inédites. Traduit du Russe par M. N..., revu par M. J. B. Eyriès. Publié avec des corrections et des notes par M. J. Klaproth. Paris: Dondey-Dupré 1827. 2 Bde.
78   Peter Perring Thoms (1791-Dez. 1855), britischer Drucker und Übersetzer. Er ging 1814 nach Macao, um im Dienste der East India Company am Druck von Morrisons Chinese-English Dictionary. Er kehrte 1825 nach England zurück. Während des 1. Opiumkrieges war er als Übersetzer für Generalmajor Gough in Kanton tätig.

César Moreau (Quelle: Wikidata)

The 2nd part of the Transactions of the Royal Asiatic Society will be published on Saturday among other papers it contains 92 rules for writing Chinese – accompanied by examples which are lithographd 8 plates[79] – I will endeavor to forward a copy for you in 2 or 3 days –

M Moreau[80] the French ViceConsul will forward this letter to Paris as it contains several enclosures.
I remain Sir Respectfully
Your Obedient Servant
Wm. Huttmann

M Jules de Klaproth

Account deliverd   6.9.3
Thomss Chinese Courtship   10.0

---

79   John Francis Davis: Eugraphia Sinensis, or, the Art of writing the Chinese character with correctness, contained in ninety-two rules and examples. To which are prefixed some observations on the Chinese writing. *Transactions of the Royal Asiatic Society* 1,2.1826, 304–312.

80   Wohl César Moreau (Marseille 1791–28. Nov. 1860), Wirtschaftsfachmann, Mitbegründer der Société Française de Statistique Universelle, Verfasser von *Über Wollhandel und Wollmanufaktur in Großbritannien von frühester bis auf gegenwärtige Zeit.* Berlin: Rücker 1929. 59 S.

Asiatic Journal January	2.9
Kingsburys Account	2.3.6
Howells ditto	1.5.0
	£ 10.10.6

M Jules de Klaproth
à Paris

140
Cornwall Place
Holloway
March 30th 1826

Sir

I very much regret that you have not yet receivd the Map of India etc. They were made up in a parcel and sent to the Asiatic Societys House for Transmission to Paris along with the Societys Transactions nearly 2 months since and until I receivd your letter of the 20th I had supposd that they had been some time in your possession – but upon enquiry I found that the Societys Clerk had neglected sending both the Transactions and your Books – They are however to be immediately sent to Mr Hearne to be forwarded to Messrs Dondey-Dupre but should any accident prevent their being sent to Mr Hearne I will forward your parcel by the Messageries Royales.

The Publishers of the Gooroo Paramartan[81] not having a waste sheet of Pages 241 and 242 the only way to obtain a complete copy is to return that you have – when a perfect one will be given in exchange for it. –

As the Map for the 2nd number[82] of your Asiatic Magazine may perhaps not be finishd for some time I should be extremely obligd by your informing me when you have occasion to write – whether the Dzang bo joins the Brahmaputra or the Irawati as most Geographers unite it to the former river and I have not succeeded in discovering their authority and feel more inclined to unite it with the latter.

Hoping to have the pleasure of soon receiving an answer to the enquiry
I remain Sir
With great respect
Your Obedient Servant
Wm Huttmann

M Jules de Klaproth
Paris

160
Royal Asiatic Societys House
Grafton Street
April 18 1826

---

81   [Constant Joseph Beschi:] *The adventures of the Gooroo Paramartan*: a tale in the Tamul language accompanied by a translation and vocabulary, together with an analysis of the first story by Benjamin Babington. London: J.M. Richardson 1822. XII,243 S.

82   Mémoire sur le cours du Yarou Dzangbo Tchou, ou du grand fleuve du Tubet; suivie de notices sur la source du Burrampouter. *Magasin asiatique* 1.1825, 302–329.

Sir

Yesterday I had the pleasure of forwarding Major Denhams Travels[83] by the Messageries Royales and I now send you the New Map of the Birman Empire – the 15th volume of the Asiatick Researches[84] is not yet ready.

I am extremely obligd by your Map of the course of the Yarou dzang bo which clearly proves that it is not connected with the Brahmaputra – I have sent a notice of the Map to the Asiatic Journal which will I doubt not be published in the Number for May

Directly the Box containing the Second volume of your Memoires arrives I will have them distributed agreeably with your request

I have the honor to be Sir

Your Obliged Servant

Wm Huttmann

M. Jules de Klaproth

à Paris

180

Royal Asiatic Societys House

Grafton Street

London Sep. 11, 1826

Sir

Mr Moreau the ViceConsul of France in England having obligingly consented to forward a Packet of letters to Paris for me I embrace the opportunity of sending you a few lines – I extremely regret that I am unable to send you a duplicate of your account as requested – I merely made memorandums of the Books sent and their prices and when the Book in which I kept those and other memoranda was full I either threw it away or allowed it to be destroyd – I applied to M Devaux for a statement of the sums paid to me on your account which he promised to send either to me or Mess.rs Lelong & Co. but I have not yet been able to obtain it –

If you have not yet arrangd the account with Mess.rs Lelong & Co I will endeavor from your letters and enquiries at MM Devaux + Rothschilds to ascertain precisely what sums I have receivd

Hoping that you have already settled with those Gentlemen in a satisfactory manner I remain Sir with great respect

Your Obligd Servant

Wm Huttmann

190

Royal Asiatic Societys House

Grafton Street London

November 13th 1826

---

83 Dixon Denham: *Narrative of travels and discoveries in Northern and Central Africa in the years 1822, 1823 and 1824, by* Major Denham, Captain Clapperton and the late Doctor Oudney, extending across the great desert to the tenth degree of Northern latitude, and from Kouka in Bornou, to Sackatoo, the capital of the Felatah. London: Murray 1826. XLVIII, 335, 269 S.

84 Band 15.1825.

Sir

We have the honor to introduce the bearer of this letter Lieutenant Colonel James Tod[85] a member of the Council and of the Committee of Correspondence of the Royal Asiatic Society who lately held the Diplomatic situation of British Political Resident in Rajpootana in the East Indies and who is now travelling through France

Any attention you may shew him will be thankfully acknowledged by us and we shall experience great pleasure in returning the compliment to such persons as may visit this Country with Letters of Introduction from you
We have the honor to be Sir
Your most Obedient Servants
Signed by order of the Committee of Cor^ce
Wm Huttmann
Secretary

à M Jules de Klaproth

210
Royal Asiatic Societys House
Grafton Street London
July 26 1827

Sir

I have the honor of informing you that a Box of Chinese Books directed to this Society but intended – as I am informed by Sir George Staunton – for you lies at the East India Companys Baggage Warehouse.

I annex a copy of Sir George Stauntons Letter relating to the Box and request to be favored with your instructions
I remain Sir
With great respect
Your very Obedient Servant
Wm Huttmann

M Jules de Klaproth

220
Copy of a Letter from Sir George Staunton

Sir George Staunton begs to furnish Mr. Huttmann with a parcel of papers respecting Mr. Klaproths Books which he requests Mr Huttmann to be so good as to forward to Mr Klaproth after all charges shall have being [Textlücke?] especially £9.19.4 the prime cost of the Books

---

85   (Islington, London 20. März 1782–18. Nov. 1835 London), Offizier der Britischen Ostindischen Kompanie (Oberstleutnant) und Orientalist. Er gab seine Stellung als politischer Agent auf, da man ihn verdächtigte, einige einheimische Fürsten über Gebühr zu begünstigen. Er kehrte 1823 nach London zurück und trat u.a. mit seinem Werk *Annals and Antiquities of Rajast'han or the Central and Western Rajpoot States of India.* Volume 1–2. London: Smith, Elder 1829, 1832 hervor.

230
Grafton Street
October 31 1827

Sir

I have the pleasure of forwarding to you a Letter from Mr Marsden in reply to that which I transmitted to him from you.

I very much regret that I am so much occupied at the present moment as to prevent my replying to your recently receivd Letters – but I will answer all the enquiries contained in them in a very few days
I remain Sir
With great respect
Your obliged and Obedient Servant
Wm Huttmann

Mr. Julius von Klaproth

240
Royal Asiatic Societys House
Grafton Street London
November 29 1827

Sir

I have the honor of returning you the thanks of the Royal Asiatic Society for your Vocabulaire etc. de la langue Georgienne[86] – Tableau du Caucase[87] and Meprises de quelques Sinologues[88] – I also request you to accept my acknowledgments for the Books you presented to me – but I regret that you should be constantly sending presents while I have not the means of making you a suitable return –

Before answering the enquiries in your recently receivd Letters I must apologise for having treated them with apparent inattention by not having replied to them earlier – My apology is that have actually not had time to sit down to write a long letter – This want of time however has arisen from temporary causes and will not I hope again prevent my paying than attention to your communications which I feel sincerely desirous of paying –

The case of Chinese Books was not even opend here although it was examined at the East India Companys Baggage Warehouse – so that I was not aware of the completeness of some of the works until I receivd your Letter of the 9th ultimo. The deficiency of the Shwuy hu tchuan[89] I can supply as I have an imperfect set of that novel in duplicate – but I regret that I have not the means of completing the I wan pi lan[90] – I wrote to my brother (who was then residing at Malacca) in 1825

---

86   *Vocabulaire et grammaire de la langue géorgienne,* Par M. J. Klaproth. Première partie. Paris: Dondey-Dupré 1827. 132 S. Teil 2 wurde posthum von M. F. Brosset veröffentlicht.

87   *Tableau historique, géographique, ethnographique et politique du Caucase et des provinces limitrophes entre la Russie et la Perse.* Paris, Leipzig: Ponthieu 1837. 187 S.

88   W. Lauterbach: Méprises singuliers de quelques sinologues. *JA* 11.1827, 113–125

89   *Shuihuzhuan* 水滸傳, der bekannte chinesische Räuberroman, in Deutschland betitelt „Die Räuber vom Liang Schan Moor".

90   *Yiwen beilan* 藝文備覽 von Sha Mu 沙木. Ausgabe 1806. 120 juan.

for a copy of that Dictionary but as he had left Malacca intending to return to Europe before my letter reached him and has not mentiond the Dictionary in any of his Letters to me I conclude that he has not got a copy of it from China – Should you however wish for another copy I will endeavor to procure it for you –

I fear that the printing of the Vocabulary in English and the Chinese dialects of Fu Këen and Keang nan is suspended as I have not heard of it for a considerable time but I will take an early opportunity of writing to Singapore or Batavia to ascertain if it is likely to be published.

The Royal Asiatic Society is in possession of some MS Singhalese Tamul vocabularies but these you have probably seen as they were for some time in the hands of M. E. Burnouf Secnd at Paris – There is also in the Societys Library a Vocabulary of the Koonawur languages consisting of the dialects Milchan Bhoteea Tartar and Theburskuds – There is also a Maldive + English Vocabulary –

You have sent me the 1st and 2nd numbers of your Magazin Asiatique but I have not the 3rd. Is it your intention to continue its publication? When your China goes to Press I hope that you will not forget that I shall feel happy in reading the Proof Sheets. –

To ensure the early delivery of your copy of the 3rd part of the Transactions of the RAS I sent it through the French Ambassador along with the copies for the Duke of Orleans and the Bibliothèque du Roi but I regret to find that there was some delay in delivering it to you – That delay must have occurred at Paris – the Council of the R As has voted you another copy of Part 1 which will be sent the first time I send you a parcel – In a former Letter I think I mentioned that any Letter or parcel addressd to G. H. Haughton Esq at J. Ruddell Todds Esq 11 John Street Adelphi London would be sure to reach him – Mr. Haughton has I know lately receivd some copies of your Table of words as he spoke to me some days since on the manner of filling it up etc. –

I have written to Dr. Wilkins to request him to allow me to purchase for you a copy of MacKerrells Carnataka Grammar[91] but have not yet receivd his answer –

The Specimens of the Scriptures printed at Serampore in 1818 is entirely out of print –

Directly I receivd your Letter of the 10th ultimo I waited on the Revd Mr Dyer[92] Secretary to the Baptist Missionary Society to propose his giving you copies of the Indian Grammars Dictionaries Bibles etc. which you have not got – in exchange for copies of your works – He instantly agreed to the proposal and promised that the Clerk should make out a List of what Books they had in duplicate that I might select what you wanted – Not hearing from him for some time a [d.i. I] called about 10 days since and found that the Clerk had neglected to make out the promised List – but he engaged to send it to me in a few days – Not having done so I have written to Mr. Dyer and expect the List immediately – I also enquired at the Bible Society for Translations into the languages of India and was promised that whatever Books cannot be obtained from the Baptist Missionary Society they will give in exchange for some of your works if they have duplicate copies – I cannot therefore make any arrangement with them until I have ascertaind what Books the Baptist Missionary Society can furnish – but as I am now more at leisure than I have been during the last three months I will endeavor to effect the exchange and forward you the Books in the course of a few days –

I will by the first conveyance send you a copy of Parburys Catalogue which I think contains some of the works you wish to procure – and after you have collected as much

---

91   *A grammar of the Carnáṭaca language* by John McKerrell, Madras: College Press 1820. 196, 15 S.
92   John Dyer (1783–1841), Nachfolger William Careys in dieser Funktion.

information for your *Mithridates*[93] as can be obtained from printed Books if you will favor me with a List of what languages you are deficient I will endeavor to obtain vocabularies of them either by writing to those individuals who are acquainted with the languages of which you want specimens or if in my power compiling them myself

Hoping that the unavoidable delay in replying to your letters has not inconvenienced you
I remain Sir
With the greatest admiration and respect
Your most Obedient Servant
Wm Huttmann

M Jules de Klaproth, Paris

PS Will you oblige me by sending the accompanying Letters to the Post office.

260

Royal Asiatic Society House
Grafton Street
January 28. 1828

Sir
I have the honor of returning you my thanks for the first number of the new series of the Journal Asiatique –

I regret that I cannot at present send you any positive information relative to the printing of your Memoir on the She Ku[94] in the Transactions of the Royal Asiatic Society – but as a Council will be summoned in a few days to take your proposal into consideration you will receive a definite answer in the early part of the ending Month – Your request relative to being allowed to have a copy of the Kunuwar Vocabularies will be taken into consideration at the same time and an official answer will be addressed to you without delay

As your copy of the 3rd part of the Transactions of the Royal Asiatic Society has by some mis chance not been receivd by you I will forward another copy of it along with Marshmans Confucius and some Books I have obtain from the Booksellers of which I enclose a list.

If the Nepal Grammar cannot be purchased would think that the Royal Asiatic Society if formally applied to would lend their copy The Ooriya Vocabulary is in the East India House Library and I fear that there is but little probability of the E I Company lending it –

I am extremely obliged by your favoring me with the 3rd Number of the Magazin Asiatique and very much regret to learn that you only intend publishing one number more – If the public patron[iz]d works according to their intrinsic merit you would certainly have had no reason to complain of not being adequately supported in the publication of that work

If you have a few minutes to spare from your important avocations I should be particularly obliged by your informing me by what process you have obtaind a character

---

93   Klaproth sammelte jahrelang Material für eine Neuausgabe des Adelungschen *Mithridates*. Die Manuskripte befanden sich im Nachlaß, jedoch sind sie heute nicht mehr nachweisbar.
94   Wohl shigu 石鼓 Steintrommeln.

with such fine strokes from a metal matrix and a wooden character – particularly stating the state of the metal when the wooden type was pressed into it to form the matrix

I enclose you a List of Books presented to the Bible Society in your name – They are more valuable than what the Society has presented to you but I considerd it best to be liberal as you may wish to obtain books from them on some future occasion –
I have still the following of your works in my
possession and wait your instructions as to their disposal – viz –
Voyage au Caucase
Memoires relatifs à l'Asie[95]
Tableaux Historiques de l'Asie[96]
Asia Polyglotta[97]
I have only obtain Marshmans Confucius from the Baptist Missionary Society out of the List of Books you wanted and have presented your Verzeichniss to them in exchange – They have however sent to me for you the following works but I will not send them to Paris till I hear from you as they do not appear to be such as you want –
Keeths Bengalee Grammar in Bengalee[98]
Sanscrit Couplets Sanscrit[99]
Euclid in Persian[100]
St Matthews Gospel Malayan[101]
Fables in Oordoo[102]
Neeticotha 3 parts Bengalee[103]
Gilchrists Oordoo Reesalah[104]
Indian Youths Magazine Anglo Bengalee[105]
Persian Reader Part 2 Anglo Persian
Yates Natural Philosophy Anglo Bengalee[106]
Rowes Hindee Spelling Book 3 parts[107]
Pleasing tales Anglo Bengalee[108]

---

95   1826, 1828.
96   *Tableaux historiques de l'Asie, depuis la monarchie de Cyrus jusqu'à nos jours, accompagnés de recherches historiques et ethnographiques sur cette partie du monde.* Avec un Atlas in-folio. Paris: Schubart 1826. 289, XXXI S. 4°
97   *Asia polyglotta.* Paris: A. Schubart 1823. XVI,384,121–144, 8 S. 4° Dazu: Sprachatlas. LIX S. 2°
98   James Keith: *A grammar of the Bengalee language.* Bālakeradigera śikṣārthe spaṣṭa praśnottara dhārāte Baṅga bhāṣāra byākaraṇa. Calcutta School-Book Society's Press 1825. 4, 75 S.
99   *A choice collection of Sanscrit couplets.* Calcutta School-Book Society's Press 1826. 88 S.
100   [Persische Übersetzung der sechs Bücher der Geographie des Euklid nach der arabischen Version des Nasī al-Dīn al Ṭousī.] Calcutta 1824. 262 S.
101   Übersetzung von Claudius Henry Thomsen, 1821.
102   *Fables in Oordoo for the use of schools.* Calcutta: Printed for the Calcutta school-book society, at the Hindoostanee press, by P. Pereira, 1819. 40 S.
103   *Fables in the Bengalee language for the use of schools* = Nīti kathā: Baṅgālā bhāṣāẏa pāṭhaśālāra nimitte. Calcutta Calcutta School-Book Society 1820-
104   [John Borthwick] Gilchrist's *Oordoo risaluh, or Rules of Hindee grammar.* Calcutta: the School book society at the Hindoostanee press, 1820. 181 S.
105   *Digdarśana: arthāt yubalokera kāraṇa samgṛhīta nānā upadeśa ... = Dig-durshun : or the Indian youth's magazine ...* Serampore 1818–1820.
106   William Yates: *Elements of natural philosophy and natural history, in a series of familiar dialogues.* Padarthabidyasara arthat balakeradigera padarthasiksarthe kathopathana. Calcutta: Calcutta School Book Soc. 1825–1832.
107   (Mrs.) Rowe: *Mūla sūtra:* Hindī bhāshā kā nausikha ke liye. Kalakattā Skūlabuka Susaiiṭi ke vāste chāpā gayā : Kalakattā ke shahara meṃ, 1820. 39 S.
108   *Pleasing tales, or, Stories designed to improve the understanding, and direct the conduct, of young persons.* Part 1 = : Manorañjanetihāsa, arthāt, Bālakadigera jñānadāẏaka o nītiśikshaka upākhyāna. Prathama bhāga. (3 Aufl.) Calcutta: Calcutta School Book Society 1828. 59 S.

Compendium of Geography Anglo Hindostanee[109]
Hindostanee Fables[110]
Ram Chondro Sormas Bengalee Vocabulary[111]
English Grammar in Bengalee[112]
Pleasing Instructor Hindostanee[113]
Pearces Geography Bengalee[114]
Stewarts Gopades Cotha – Anglo Bengalee[115]
Malay Hymns – Roman character[116]
Dialogues on Geography etc. Anglo Bengalee[117]
Should you wish to have these Books I will forward them to Paris directly I hear from you on the subject and send any of the works you may mention to the Society in exchange – or if you wish it I will return them to the Society

I have the honor of enclosing you some Prospectusses of the Oriental Translation Committee and I shall be particularly obliged by your permitting the accompanying Letters to be forwarded to the individuals to whom they are addressed

Since writing thus far a Council has been summoned for the 2nd of February to consider your application – I will therefore delay your packet till that day that I may be able to send you an answer relative to the She Ku [石鼓][118] and the Kunuwar Vocabularies

Regretting that I have not been more successful in obtaining Books for you in the Indian dialects
I remain Sir
With great respect
Your Obliged + Obedient Servant
Wm Huttmann

Mr. Jules de Klaproth, Paris

280
Royal Asiatic Societys House
Grafton Street
London Feb 2 1828

Sir

---

109 *A compendium of geography, Hindostanee and English.* Calcutta: School Book Press 1824. 147 S.
110 nicht ermittelt.
111 Ram Chondro Sorma [Rāmacandra Śarmā]: *Vocabulary of the Bengalee language.* Calcutta 1820. 516 Sp.
112 Iṃreji bhāshāra byākaraṇa. *A grammar of the English language; for the use of natives of Bengal.* By J. D. Pearson, Superintendent of the Hon. Company's Bengalee schools. Cacutta: Calcutta School Book Society 1820. 8, 103 S.
113 ? *The pleasing instructor. A selection of moral and entertaining pieces.* Calcutta 1824. 92 S. (Urdu)
114 William Hopkins Pearce: *Bhūgola bṛttānta.* Calcutta: Calcutta School Book Society 1822.
115 Charles Stewart: *Oopodes cotha [or Moral tales of history].* Calcutta: Calcutta School Book Society 1820. 4, 68 S.
116 Nur ermittelt Ausg. Singapore 1846: *Puji pujian, dan tahlil, yang dilagukan pada kutika sambahyang.*
117 John Thomas Graves: *Dialogues on geography, astronomy &c. for the use of schools.* Calcutta: Calcutta School Book Society 1824. 160 S.
118 Die Abhandlung über die Steintrommel-Inschriften wurde bisher nicht ermittelt.

I have the honor of transmitting to you the decisions of the Council of this Society relative to your Memoir on the She Ku and to your being furnished with a copy of the Kunawar Vocabularies –

As the number of copies of each plates of the Inscriptions and texts wanted for the Societys Transactions will be 750 I proposed that Fifty pounds should be voted for them instead of £39 – which would have been about the expense of 500 copies

I very much regret that the Council cannot engage to publish your Memoir until they have seen it but I have the fullest confidence in their ordering it to be printed when it is submitted to them – and I have therefore expressed that idea in the accompanying resolution

You have not mentiond whether your Memoir would be written in French or in English but that is not very material as if you send it in French I should feel a pleasure in translating it for you –

It not being finally settled whether the Kunawar + Maldive Vocabularies will be printed in the 3rd Volume of the Societys Transactions or not a conclusive answer to your request for copies of them cannot be returned but if the Council decides on not printing them I will endeavor to get permission to have them transcribed for you and have no doubt of success[119] –

I remain Sir

With great respect

Your most Obedient Servant

Wm Huttmann

M Jules de Klaproth

290

At a Meeting of the Council of the Royal Asiatic Society held on Saturday the 2nd day of February 1828

It was Resolved

That Mr. Klaproth be informed that this Society confiding in his high reputation as a Chinese Scholar will defray the expense (to the extent of Fifty pounds) of lithographing 750 copies of each of the plates connected with the She Ku – but that the Council is prevented by its constitution from pledging itself to the publication of a memoir before it is submitted to its inspection but entertains little doubt that when it sees the memoir its publication in the Societys Transactions will be approved

Also that Mr. Klaproth be informed that as the Society has some intention of printing the Kunuwar + Maldive Vocabularies in its Transactions the Council is unable to let Mr. Klaproth have copies of them at present

Wm Huttmann

300

Royal Asiatic Societys House

Grafton Street London

February 29 1828

Sir

---

119   Diese Vokabulare wurden offenbar nicht in den Transactions abgedruckt. Das Material wurde insofern freigegeben, eine Publikation Klaproths war indes nicht festzustellen. Vgl. Brief 360.

On the day I was honored with your Letter of the 9th Instant I forwarded by the Messageries Royales all the Books I had obtaind for you and hope that they have long since been receivd –

Directly I heard that you would accept the Books sent by the Baptist Missionary Society I sent the remainder of the parcel you sent to me – with the exception of Asia Polyglotta – to that Society but have not yet receivd their acknowledgment of the receipt of them – I enclose a Letter from the Bible Society which I suppose contains thanks for the Books presented to them in your name

It is impossible to obtain a copy of the Bhotanta Dictionary Grammar lately published by Mr. Carey[120] – One of my Correspondents at Selenginsk lately requested me to send him some information and Books elating to the language of Tibet – I therefore endeavord to get a copy of the Bhotanta Dictionary to send him but was unsuccessful –

I am extremely obliged by your details relating to cutting Chinese type and unhappy to find that the plan which I had assumed to be practicable is that which is really adopted at Paris – At the time I receivd the number of your Magazine Asiatique which contains the article on the Dzang bo I read it with real interest and pleasure and can state positively from having translated the texts you quote and compared them with the original Mandchu map in the East India House Library – that you was [!] fully warranted

in unequivocally asserting that the Yarou Dzang bo tchou[121] does not join the Burrumpooter but enters China under the name of Pin lang Keang[122] and from thence flows into Ava –

As I have heard that an article on the Burrumpooter that appeared in the Oriental Herald some months since and in which you was [!] attackd – has been attributed to me – I take the liberty of stating that I was not the author – Indeed I scarcely ever contribute articles to Magazines my time being too fully occupied to afford leisure for writing anonymous articles – if even I did not disapprove of the practice of making assertions and attacks to which the author would not affix his name

Hoping you will excuse the hurries manner in which this letter is written
I remain
Sir
With great respect
Your Obliged and Obedient Servant
Wm Huttmann

Mr. Julius von Klaproth
Paris

320
Royal Asiatic Societys House
Grafton Street London
May 1 1828
Sir

---

120   *A dictionary of the Bhotanta or Boutan language*, printed from a manuscript copy made by the late Rev. Frederic Christian Gotthelf Schroeter, edited by J. Marshman. To which is prefixed a grammar of the Bhotanta language. Serampore 1826. III, 45 S.

121   Der Tsangpo entspringt in der Nähe des Kailash, fließt nach Osten durch Tibet, bis er nach Süden abknickt und in der Folge sich westwärts wendet, um teils unter dem Namen Brahmaputra schließlich in Bangladesh ins Meer zu münden. Dieser Nachweis wurde indes erst 1913 von F. M. Bailey geführt.

122   Der Binlang Jiang (Irrawaddy) entspringt in Tibet, fließt aber dann nordsüdlich durch Burma (Myanmar).

I have the honor of returning you the thanks of the Royal Asiatic Society for your donation of a Memoir on the Sources of the Brahmaputra etc. and for Mr. Lauterbach (i.e. Klaproths) critique on Mr. Schotts works of Confucius[123] –

Major General Symons this morning returned your collection of words translated into Teloogoo and I have the [sure] of enclosing it for you – I translated the List into English because the General does not read French

I have forwarded your work on the Brahmaputra and Mr. Lauterbachs publication to the Editor of the Asiatic Journal and forward you a Letter I receivd from that Gentleman on the 18th ultimo – I have marked out his name as he wishes to be incognito

I very much regret having to report that it is not possible to procure a copy of the Bhotanta Dictionary in London If you wish for it particularly – I can write to Calcutta for one of you have no correspondent there

I shall be particularly obliged by your allowing the accompanying Letters to be sent to the Post offices and remain
In great haste
Your very Obedient Servant
Wm Huttmann

Monsieur Jules de Klaproth

330
PS I have forwarded the packet for the Asiatic Society of Calcutta to the Society, Agent in London and have had the pleasure of seeing Dr. Rosen 2 or three times since he reached London

340
Royal Asiatic Societys House
Grafton Street London
July 1 1828

Sir
I have the honor of returning you thanks from the Royal Asiatic Society for your Review of Schroeters Dictionary Principles of the affinity of languages etc. and request you to accept my personal thanks for copies of the same works –

No opportunity has yet presented itself for offering the collection of Chinese coins to any institution or individual which is likely to purchase them but I hope in a few days to see a person who may probably be inclined to buy them.

Although the Kunuwar Vocabularies were referrd some months ago since to a Gentlemen for his opinion as to their being adapted for publication in the Transactions of the Royal Asiatic Society – he has not yet formally reported his opinion, but I calculate on his reporting against their being printed – Directly he does so I will propose to the Council that you shall be furnished with copies of them

I shall be particularly obliged by your having the enclosed letters sent to the Post office and
I remain Sir
With great respect and esteem

---

123   *Dr. Wilhelm Schott's vorgebliche Übersetzung der Werke des Confucius aus der Ursprache.* Eine literarische Betrügerei, dargestellt von Wilhelm Lauterbach. Leipzig, Paris: Ponthieu 1828. 70 S.

Your Obliged and Obedient Servant
Wm Huttmann

360

Royal Asiatic Societys House
Grafton Street London
July 7 1828

Sir

On Saturday the Council of the Royal Asiatic Society decided on not printing the collection of Kunuwar Vocabularies in the Societys Transactions – I therefore proposed that you should be allowed to have it copied for printing or any other purpose and have now the pleasure of sending it to you
Hoping to be favord with it as soon as you can possibly get it transcribed
I remain – Sir –
With great respect
Your Obliged and Obedient Servant
Wm Huttmann

M. Jules de Klaproth

370

Royal Asiatic Societys House
Grafton Street London
September 1 1828

Sir

I regret that I cannot in compliance with your request inform you the price of Mr. Wilsons account of the Burmese war[124] as no copies of that work have reached London

Coll. Kennedy[125] resides at Bombay so that I fear it will not be possible to obtain a copy of his work on languages in exchange for the copy of your Asia Polyglotta which I have in trust for you –

I am very sorry that you have been obliged to discontinue the Magazin Asiatique as it furnished so much valuable information relating to Central Asia which is a part of the world in which I feel much interested

Directly I receivd from you M de Hammers answer to M Senkowski[126] I handed it to the Editor of the Asiatic Journal who has inserted the substance of it in the Journal for this month

I am very happy to find that you have resumd the printing of the Mandchu Dictionary and have added the Mandchu characters – I am also much pleased with the specimen of

---

124   H. H. Wilson: *Documents illustrative of the Burmese war: with an introductory sketch of the events of the war and an appendix.* Calcutta: Government Gazette Press 1827. 92, 248, 93 S.

125   Wohl Vans Kennedy (1784–1846), schottischer Generalmajor der britischen Armee, Beamter der East India Company, Sanskritist und Iranist. Seit 1817 fungierte er als Generalanwalt der Armee in Bombay.

126   Joseph von Hammer-Purgstall: Réponse à la lettre de Tutundju-Oglou. *NJA* 2.1828, 50–71 Sonderdruck) 24 S. Józef Sękowski hatte Hammers Sur les origines russes kritisiert. Vgl. *Lettre de Tutundju-Oglou-Moustafa-Aga, véritable philosophe turk, à M. Thaddée Bulgarin, Rédacteur de l'Abeille du Nord.* St. Petersburg: Gretsch 1828. 76 S.

your Comparative Vocabulary and you may feel assured that if any opportunity for obtaining lists of words for you, presents itself – I shall avail myself of it with pleasure –

Requesting you will have Coll. Briggs[127] translation of Farishta[128] and Coll Tods Annals of Rajasthan announced in the Journal Asiatique

I remain Sir
With great respect
Your Obliged Servant
Wm Huttmann

PS Will you oblige me by having the accompanying letters put into the Post office –

380
Royal Asiatic Societys House
Grafton Street London
September 30 1828

Sir
I regret having to inform you that through the absence of the Librarians to the British Museum the Japanese Map of the world cannot be found at present – I will however apply there again in a few days when I hope that either some of the Librarians will have returned or I shall be able to find it without their assistance

I submitted your proposal to Mess[rs] Howell + Stewart and enclose their reply but expect to have a more definite answer in a few days – which I will forward to you without delay

Having a duplicate of the report of the Proceedings of the Literary Society of Bombay I forward it to you under the impression that you may like to extract some parts of it for the Journal Asiatique –

I have on 2 or 3 occasions taken the liberty of enclosing in your packet letters for persons not resident in France – It has however occurred to me that my doing so may have put you to the expense of paying postage for them. Should it be necessary in France to pay the postage of Letters for Italy + Germany on their being put into the Post office at Paris – I shall be obliged by your informing me so when you have occasion to writing –

I have the honor to be
Sir – With great respect
Your very Obedient Servant
Wm Huttmann

390
Royal Asiatic Societys House
Grafton Street
October 3 1828

---

127   A. J. A.: Briggs, John (1785–1875). *Dictionary of National Biography*. London: Smith, Elder & Co. 1885–1900. Bd. 6.

128   Muḥammad Qāsim Hindū-Šāh Astarābādī Firišta: *History of the rise of the Mahomedan power in India, till the year A.D.* 1612; to which is added an account of the conquest, by the kings of Hydrabad, of those parts of the Madras provinces denominated the Ceded districts and northern Circars. Translated from the original Persian of Mahomet Kasim Ferishta, by John Briggs. London: Spottiswoode 1829.

Sir

The two letters that were lost were of no consequence and I have sent duplicates of them Your answer to the Editor of the Asiatic Journal is inserted in the number that accompanies this Letter – it is also published in the Oriental Herald

The Revd. W. Forshall[129] in whose care it was supposed by the Assistants at the British Museum the Japanese Map of the world was – did not return to his post till the 28th and I yesterday found an examined the Map – Its title is 王國總界圖 and it was printed at 江戶 in 貞享 5th year[130] – the coloring however is very different from that which you sent me – for instead of each quarter of the world being uniform in color – the different divisions of each quarter have different colors – for example – Japan is light red China yellow Corea light red – Tartary Green India white etc.[131]

Regretting that I could not obtain this information for you sooner

I remain Sir

With Sincere respect

Your Obliged Servant

Wm Huttmann

400

Royal Asiatic Societys House
Grafton Street London
November 12 1828

Sir

On the 4th Instant I forwarded a parcel to you by the Messageries Royales which I hope has been duly receivd – A letter would have been enclosed in it requesting you to have the copies of Baron Humboldts Essay I took the liberty of enclosing – delivered – but that I feared it might occasion the detention of the parcel at the Custom House – You will I hope pardon my apparent rudeness –

I regret that I cannot get a definitive answer from Mess[rs] Howell + Stewart relative to the Chrestomathie Mandchou and I do not think that they will be able to decide for some days as the partnership is in an unsettled state at present –

Your account of the Japanese Map of the world would have been translated and sent to the Oriental Herald before this time had I not considered it best to wait to give you an opportunity of making any alterations or additions you may consider necessary from my Letter of the 30th Ultimo –

The 1st fasciculus of the 2nd volume of the transactions of the Royal Asiatic Society is nearly ready for publication and I hope to have the pleasure of sending you a copy by the end of the year

---

129 Wohl vielmehr Josiah Forshall (29. März 1795–18. Dez. 1863), Bibliothekar am British Museum, 1827–1837 Leiter der Handschriftenabteilung, ab 1829 auch Kaplan am Foundling Hospital. Vgl. *Dictionary of National Biography* 1885–1900. Band 20, S. 11.

130 Jōkyō 5 = 1688

131 Vgl. *NJA* 2.1828, 400, mit Zitat aus diesem Brief. Die Karte, berichtigter Titel: 萬國總界圖 Bankoku sōkai zu, ist datiert 1688 und wurde von Engelbert Kaempfer aus Japan mitgebracht; sie befindet sich im British Museum (British Library). Autoren waren Ishikawa Toshiyuki Ryūsen 石川流宣 (†1715) und Sagamiya Tahai (Verleger).

I remain Sir
With Sincere Respect
Your Obliged and Obedient Servant
Wm Huttmann

420
Royal Asiatic Societys House
Grafton Street
London Dec 1 1828

Sir
I have the honor of requesting that you will oblige Coll Tod by paying his subscription for 1828 and 1829 to the Societe Asiatique – and on your informing me what sum you have paid I will either remit it to you or credit it on your account

Coll T has requested me to apologize for troubling you with this commission and to return his thanks for your announcement of his Annals of Rajasthan –
I remain Sir
With Great Respect
Your very Obedient Servant
Wm Huttmann

Monsieur Jules de Klaproth

430
Royal Asiatic Societys House
Grafton Street London
December 16 1828

Sir
I have the honor of returning you my thanks and the thanks of the Royal Asiatic Society for several of your publications that have lately been receivd –

The rapidity with which your works follow each other excites the greatest surprise here – indeed some people almost imagine you can live without sleep or relaxation

I am most obliged By the Chinese coins you sent me and have sent a few of Yung chings [雍正] Kea Kings [嘉慶] and Taou Kwangs [道光] – I regret that they are not fine specimens but they are the best I have – Any coins in my possession are at your service –

I regret my inability to inform you who wrote the attack on the Orientalists of Paris but should I learn who is the author I shall immediately inform you

The article on the commerce of Russia with China and the account of the Japanese Map were sent to the Oriental Herald at the beginning of the Month

I am sincerely gratified by the intelligence that the King of France has subscribed 3000 francs per annum to the Asiatic Society of Paris – as it was much to be regretted that a Society whose Members were so eminent for their knowledge and preeminent for their zeal and industry should experience a want of funds and a consequent inability to publish many valuable works
I remain Sir
With Sincere Respect

Your Obedient and Obliged Servant
Wm Huttmann

PS The 1st part of the Second Volume of our Transactions will be published in [...]
How shall I send your Copy?

450
Royal Asiatic Societys House
Grafton Street London
February 2 1829

Sir
Colonel Tod has requested me today that he will be particularly obliged by your paying his subscription to the Societe Asiatique for the year 1829 – I have credited your account 2-10-0 for the 2 years subscriptions

Colonel FitzClarence[132] also would be much obliged by your paying his arrears and present years subscription and I will repay you

I fear that the Oriental Translation Committee will not subscribe for your Chrestomathie Mandchou[133] as it has repeatedly refused similar applications on the ground of their object being to encourage the making of translations not to purchase copies of those that are already made

Dr. Wilkins has certainly receivd the 3 volumes of your Memoires as he mentiond to me you having dedicated it to him and appeard to be gratified by your having done so – I conclude that his not having written to you has arisen from his great age and his not having been very well lately –

In relation to your history of Georgia that would come strictly within the limits of the Oriental Translation Fund and there is not the smallest doubt that you would have one of the pecuniary rewards for your translation but the Committee cannot pledge themselves to print or give a reward for a translation unless it is submitted to them for examination – Would you translate it (and you might confidently depend on a reward for your labor) it would be best to have the translation made into English under your own superintendence at Paris –

About the description of Tibet I fear there may be a little difficulty but as the work would be both interesting and valuable I would endeavor to answer any technical objections to its publication by the Committee –

The opinions I have given in reference to the Oriental Translation Committee are not given Ex Officio but privately
I have the honor to be Sir
With sincere admiration + respect
Your Obliged + Obedient Servant
Wm Huttmann

---

132   George FitzClarence, Earl of Munster (London 29. Jan. 1794–20. März 1842 London), Generalmajor, 1841–1842 Präsident der Royal Asiatic Society. Er war besonders um die Publikation orientalischer Texte bemüht und fungierte zeitweise als Vizepräsident des Oriental Translation Fund. Vgl. *Dictionary of national biography* 7.1921/22, 106–107.

133   *Chrestomathie mandchou ou Recueil de textes mandchou, destiné aux personnes qui veulent s'occuper de l'étude de cette langue.* Paris: Impr. royale 1828. XII, 275 S.

PS Several numbers of the Calcutta Quarterly Oriental Magazine have lately been receivd in London if you wish to complete your set I will forward them to you on your informing me which is the last number you have receivd

470

Royal Asiatic Societys House
Grafton Street
London Feb 9 1829

Sir

I am directed by the Oriental Translation Committee to express to you the high gratification they have felt in reading your Letter relating to the Translation of a history of Georgia and a description of Tibet

The history of Georgia will they anticipate be considered by the Literary world an extremely valuable work and they will feel a real pleasure in being the channel through which it is communicated to the public But while they are certain that your translation will be approved and printed

and a reward conferrd on the translator they are prevented by their regulations from pledging themselves to the publication of any work or fixing the amount of reward for it before the translation is submitted to them for inspection

The exclusive object of the Committee being the publication of translations it will be necessary that the text of your description of Tibet etc. should be limited to translations from Chinese Mandchu etc. But this arrangement will not exclude any of the information you have collected as that may appear in an introduction or appendix and in the form of Notes – A good Map of Tibet and Western Chinese Tartary would be a valuable addition to the work

In relation to your Chrestomathie Mandch[o]u the Committee has directed me to express their regret that their rules preclude them from complying with your request and add that they have several times been under disagreeable necessity of refusing similar applications
I have the honor to be Sir
With great respect
Your very Obedient Servant
Wm Huttmann
Secretary

490

London March 2 1829
Sir
I very much regret learning that you have not receivd your copy of the 1st part of the 2nd Volume of the Transactions of the Royal Asiatic Society – It was sent to you some weeks since through the Foreign Office under cover to Hamilton C Hamilton Esq Secretary of Embassy Paris – I the more regret the delay that has occurred in its delivery on account of its containing a Letter from Mr Marsden to you about which that Gentleman enquired yesterday and also a

Letter to Dondey Dupre relative to the copies of the Transactions that were sent to him

–

In relation to Monsieur Abel Remusats copy I should be extremely obliged by your in forming that Gentleman that it was enclosed in the packet addressd to Dondey-Dupre with a Band on it directed "Monsieur Abel Remusat Paris" This band I suppose must by some accident have been lost as Dondey Dupre acknowledges the receipt of seven copies while only 6 were intended for him – He will therefore deliver the seventh copy to Mons. Remusats order –

It was certainly not intended that Dondey Dupre should charge the expenses on the copies delivered to the Members of this Society who reside at Paris but that he should take credit for them in his account –

The missing packet contains – if I remember right – copies of Colonel Tods papers for you and should it not have been receivd before this letter reaches you – I will immediately on receiving your reply endeavor to trace it and get it forwarded to you without further delay

I have the honor to be Sir

With the greatest respect

Your very Obliged and Obedient Servant

Wm Huttmann

510

Royal Asiatic Societys House

Grafton Street London

March 27. 1829

Sir

I have the pleasure of presenting to you through Colonel Briggs a Member of the Oriental Translation Committee the Travels of Ibn Batuta [134] which is the first work that Committee has published

Colonel Briggs whom I have the pleasure of introducing to you will be able to give you any information relative to the Committee you may wish to obtain – in case you intend noticing it in any French Periodical

I have the honor to be Sir

With great respect

Your very Obedient Servant

Wm Huttmann

Secretary

Monsr Klaproth

520

Mr. Huttmann does not know who translated Mr. Klaproth[s] paper on the introduction of Chinese writing into Japan

---

134 Muḥammad Ibn-ʿAbdallāh Ibn-Baṭṭūṭa, 1304–1377: The travels of Ibn Batuta. Translated from the abridged Arabic manuscript copies, preserved in the public library of Cambridge with notes, illustrative of the history, geography, botany, antiquities, &c. occurring throughout the work, by the Rev. Samuel Lee. London: Printed for the Oriental Translation Committee 1829. XVIII, 243 S.

530

Royal Asiatic Societys House
Grafton Street London
April 1 1829

Sir

I have the pleasure of informing you that the Oriental Translation Committee has consented to the publication of your history of Georgia and Description of Tibet in French – and that it does not require the sight of the original Georgian of your History

Some days since I had the pleasure of sending to you Colonel Briggs the very first copy (excepting that for the Societe Asiatique which was sent at the same time) of Ibn Batuta that was put into circulation

Sir William Ouseley[135] has exchanged the plates to the first Volume of his history of Persia for your Chrestomathie Mandchou and as I sent them by Colonel Briggs I hope they have been in your possession for several days

Monsieur Persuch [?] having been Secretary to Sir Sidney Smith[136] if the Letters for him are sent to that Gentlemans Hotel they will I doubt not reach their destination

I sincerely hope that you have long ere this received the missing fasciculus of the Transactions of the Royal Asiatic Society particularly as several Letters accompanied it – Should it not have been deliverd to you yet I shall be particularly obliged by your writing to me immediately on the subject

In your Letter of the 13th Ultimo you mention having sent the number of the Universel[137] that contains the critique on Mr Schmidts Mongol history – but unfortunately it was not enclosed in your packet – I will send it if you favor me with a copy – to the Asiatic Journal to which I have forwarded your account of M de Hammers

Ottoman History

I very much regret that there are not in this Library any materials relating to the altitudes of Asiatic mountains but what are printed and very generally known

If possible I will borrow some numbers of the Canton Gazette for you for a few weeks
I have the honor to be Sir
In great haste
but with great respect
Your very Obliged and Obedient Servant
Wm Huttmann
Monsieur Jules de Klaproth
Paris

550

Grafton Street London
April 10 1829

Mr Huttmann has the honor of forwarding to Monsʳ Klaproth a duplicate of the first fasciculus of the 2nd Volume of the Transactions of the Royal Asiatic Society but

---

135 William Ouseley (Monmouthshire 1767–1842 Boulogne-sur-Mer), britischer Orientalist; er beschäftigte sich hauptsächlich mit Persien.

136 Sir Sidney Smith (Westminster 21. Juni 1764–26. Mai 1840 Paris), britischer Admiral. Er kämpfte auf britischer Seite gegen die aufständischen Kolonien sowie gegen Napoleon. Anschließend lebte er meist in Paris.

137 *L'Universel* wurde in Paris 1829–1830 von J. P. Abel-Rémusat und Antoine Saint-Martin, dem Historiker und Armeniologen, herausgegeben. Als Geschäftsführer fungierte Clerc de Landresse.

sincerely hope that the missing packet may still be receivd as it containd several Letters for Monsr Klaproth and other persons

560
Royal Asiatic Societys House
Grafton Street London
July 1 – 1829

Sir

I have the pleasure of forwarding to you the 2nd Report of the Oriental Translation Committee in which your works on Georgia and Tibet are announced

The specimen of the 8vo Basiles Dictionary[138] affords me much satisfaction – such a manageable volume is very much needed and the abundance of abridged variants and synonymous characters it promises to furnish will make it peculiarly valuable

I shall be particularly obliged by your allowing your Servant to take the accompanying Letters to the Post office and remain Sir
With Sincere Respect
Your very Obliged + Obedient Servant
Wm Huttmann

M Jules de Klaproth

570
Royal Asiatic Societys House
Grafton Street
London July 16. 1829

Sir

I have the pleasure of returning you the thanks of the Royal Asiatic Society for your account of the Egyptian Alphabet and of sending you the 2nd Report of the Oriental Translation Committee

I am quite ashamed of troubling you so frequently with Letters etc. but hope that you will obligingly have them sent to the Post office
I have the honor to be Sir
With great respect
Your obliged & Obedient Servant
Wm Huttmann

Monsr Jules de Klaproth
Paris

580
Royal Asiatic Societys House
Grafton Street London
August 29 1829

---

138 Die Société asiatique plante zu dieser Zeit eine „Taschenausgabe" des chinesischen Lexikons von Basile Brollos Wörterbuch: Doch der Erfolg von Morrisons und der Rückzug von Heinrich Kurz aus der Sinologie beendeten das Projekt.

Dear Sir

I extremely regret learning that Monsr Dondey Dupre has omitted delivering the packets forwarded to him for that purpose – I now enclose a Letter requesting him to deliver them immediately –

In a packet I shall send in a few days to Colonel Briggs 51 Rue de Vaugirard I shall have the pleasure of enclosing for you the Memoirs of Jehangeer[139], the Travels of Macarius[140] and Mr Daviss Tragedy[141] of which I have received your review

I have sent the notice of W. Greppos[142] work to the Editor of the Asiatic Journal and offerd him the use of your observations on the Hieroglyphical Alphabet

Your Letter addressd to Messrs Longman + Co. has been deliverd and if an answer is sent I will forward it to you without delay

I have taken the liberty of enclosing in your packet some Letters of thanks from the Asiatic Society of Bengal and

I remain Dear Sir

With sincere respect

Your very Obliged + Obed Serv

Wm Huttmann

600

London October 6 1829

Sir

I have taken the liberty of addressing the accompanying packet to you shall be extremely obliged by your supporting the request addressd to Mons Jomard[143]

I have the honor to be Sir

With sincere respect

Your very Obliged + Obedient Serv[t]

Wm Huttmann

Monsieur Jules de Klaproth

Paris

W Murray has not replied to your letter yet but I believe that he is out of town

610

Royal Asiatic Society House

Grafton Street London

November 23 1829

Sir

---

139   Jahangir: *Memoirs of the emperor Jahangueir*, written by himself and translated from a Persian manuscript, by major David Price. London: Oriental Translation Comittee 1829. IV, 141 S.

140   *The travels of Macarius, Patriarch of Antioch.* London: Oriental Translation Fund 1829. 9 Teile in 2 Bdn. Übersetzung von: Safrat al-batrīk Makārijūs al-Ḥalabī bi-qalam w̄aladihī aš-šammās Būlus.

141   John Francis Davis: *Han Koong Tsew, or The Sorrows of Han.* A Chinese tragedy. London: Murray 1829. 18 S.

142   J. G. H. Greppo: *Essay on the hieroglyphic system of M. Champollion, Jr., and on the advantages which it offers to sacred criticism.* Boston: Perkins & Marvin 1830. XII, 276 S.

143   Edmé François Jomard (Versailles 22. Nov. 1777–23. Sept. 1862 Paris), französischer Ägyptologe, seit 1828 Bibliothekar an der Königlichen Bibliothek.

I have the pleasure of forwarding to you from the Oriental Translation Committee Mr Daviss Translations of the Haou kew chuen[144]

The Asiatic Journal was sent as usual to the Foreign office on the 1st of this month and I very much regret learning that it had not reached Paris when your wrote your last note – It has however – I hope – reached you ere this time – Mr. Murray has not yet replied to your letter and I do not recollect having sent any thing with the Asiatic Journal so that if the packet

does not come to hand I can easily repair the loss

Your notices of Tibet and Peking will I doubt not be very acceptable to the Editor of the Asiatic Journal to whom I have forwarded them

Mr Crawford the author of the History of the Indian Archipelago[145] asked me last week if your Description of China was published and I informed him that it was not and that I feared a long time might elapse before it appeared I am however very agreeably surprised at reading in your account of the Plan of Peking that it is in the Press

I shall be particularly obliged by your having the accompanying packet forwarded to Coll Briggs

I have the honor to be Sir

With great respect

Your very Obedient Servant

Wm Huttmann

630
Royal Asiatic Societys House
Grafton Street London
February 1 1830

Dear Sir

I very much regret that through the illness of Sir Gore Ouseley[146] your offer to edit a translation of the History of Japan has not been taken into consideration yet – but as he is getting better I sincerely hope that the Committee will soon meet and your proposal agreed to –

I shall be extremely grateful by the appearance of the annals of Japan[147] under the auspices of the Oriental Translation Committee as I think it would be interesting to very many and am certain that it would be edited and elucidated in the most satisfactory manner

I remain Dear Sir

With great respect

Your very Obliged + Obedient Servant

Wm Huttmann

---

144 John Francis Davis: *The fortunate union; a romance;* in two volumes; to which is added a Chinese tragedy. London: Oriental Translation Fund 1829. 2 Bde. [Haoqiuzhuan]

145 John Crawfurd: *History of the Indian archipelago containing an account of the manners, arts, languages, religions, institutions, and commerce of its inhabitants.* Edinburgh: Constable 1820. 3 Bde.

146 Gore Ouseley (Limerick 24. Juni 1770–18. Nov. 1844 Hall Barn Park), britischer Diplomat und Orientalist. Er war 1810–1814 Botschafter in Teheran.

147 *Nipon o dai itsi ran, ou Annales des empereurs du Japon, traduites par M. Isaac Titsingh avec l'aide de plusieurs interprètes attachés au comptoir hollandais de Nangasaki:* ouvrage revu, complété et corrigé sur l'original japonois-chinois, accompagné des notes, et précédé d'un aperçu de l'Histoire du Japon par M. J. Klaproth. Paris: Oriental Translation Fund; sold by Parberry, Allen & Co. 1834. VIII, XXXVI,460 S. – Übersetzung des *Nippon ōdai ichiran* 日本王代一覽 des Hayashi Shunsai 林春齋 (1618–1680).

Monsr Klaproth, Paris

640
London Feb 17 1830
Sir
Having this evening receivd a packet addressd to you – which may probably be that you expected from Mr Tourgeneff[148] – I hasten to forward it to you – in compliance with your request –

I have sent Potockis Voyages[149] and the Gazette Litteraire to the Editor of the Asiatic Journal and have no doubt that he will review the Counts work –

Both on your account and on that of the Oriental Translation Committee I very much regret that the history of Armenia has been translated into French at St Petersburg

On the receipt of your Letter of the 12th Instant I called at Parbury & Cos to propose that they should take 20 copies of your Chrestomathie Mandchou in exchange for Johnsons Edition of Richardsons Persian Dictionary[150] – As neither of the Partners was at home I left a written memorandum and directly I receive an answer from them I will forward it to you

When Colonel Tod comes to town I will mention your proposed exchange to him and the first time I see Sir G. Staunton – which will probably be in 2 or 3 days – I will enquire about your Chinese Books –

We have only receivd 3 numbers of the Canton Register but it is probable that Sir G. Staunton has more and if so I will endeavor to borrow them for you

Your name shall be placed on the list of subscribers to the Chinese Grammar and Dictionary that is to be printed at Macao

I will endeavor to get some information for you relating to the Chinese trade at Canton ad interim – I send the last number of the Quarterly Review and a tract on Chinese trade both written by Servants of the East India Company
I have the honor to be Sir
With great respect
Your very Obliged + Obedient Servant
Wm Huttmann

660
Royal Asiatic Societys House
Grafton St Bond St
London March 15 1830

Sir

---

148 Aleksandr Ivanovič Turgenev (7. Apr. 1784–15. Dez. 1845 Moskau), Ministerialbeamter und Historiker. Nach seinem Studium betrat er die Beamtenlaufbahn, verkehrte aber viel mit Literaten (so war er ein enger Freund Puschkins) und stellte sich in Gegensatz zum Regime Zar Alexander I., der ihn 1824 aller Ämter enthob. Nach 1825 lebte er meist im Ausland. Von Zar Nikolaus I. wurde er mit der Sammlung von Materialien zur Geschichte Rußlands beauftragt. Vgl. Brokgauz/Efron 34.1901, 96.

149 *Voyage dans les steps d'Astrakhan et du Caucase.* Histoire primitive des peuples qui ont habité anciennement ces contrées. Nouveau périple du Pont-Euxin, par le comte J. Potocki, membre des Sociétés asiatiques de Paris, de Londres et de Bombay. Paris: Merlin 1829. 2 Bde.

150 John Richardson (1741–1812): *A dictionary, Persian, Arabic and English; with a dissertation on the languages, literature, and manners of Eastern nations.* A new edition, considerably enlarged by Francis Johnson. London: Parbury, Allen & Co. 1829. LXXXVI, 9, 1714 S.

I have the pleasure of informing you that the Oriental Translation Committee has agreed to your proposal that the History of Japan should be printed at Paris at its expenses –
The Committee has directed me to mention that its regulations and practice will not allow it to unite with any person in the expense of printing any work but that the whole of the impression must be at its disposal. It would however probably order such additional number of copies to be printed as you think it likely would be sold in France and Germany – The number required in England would be 500 and I shall be particularly obliged by your informing me how many copies above that number should be printed –

As the Committee has generally had its historical works printed in 4to it has directed me to enquire if you have any objection to that form – and to request that you will oblige me with an estimate of printing a sheet in 6vo and one in 4to – and that you will favor me with an approximate estimate of the number of 4to or 8vo sheets the whole work is likely to make

I am particularly desirous that such a Map as you can furnish should accompany the annals – but the Committee appears to fear that it will be too expensive – Will you therefore oblige me with information what the expense of engraving or lithographing

it would be – and how much per hundred the impressions would cost including paper –

As I should feel much gratified by learning that the work was in the press – I take the liberty of requesting that you will favor me with an answer to enquiries containd in the preceding part of this Letter as soon as your convenience permits – and I will take the very earliest opportunity of submitting your letter to the Committees consideration

May I take the liberty of requesting that you will pay 25 Francs for me to the Societe Française de Statistique Universelle and allow your Servant to put the accompanying Letters in the Post office

I have the pleasure of sending you a separate copy of the Essay on Chinese Poetry from Mr Davis[151] accompanied by a Letter

I very much regret that the History of Georgia should have been published at St Petersburg which prevents the appearance of your translation but I hope that nothing will occur to prevent the account of Tibet being printed under the auspices of the Oriental Translation Committee

Coll Tod has requested me to mention that he will feel much pleasure in exchanging a set of his Rajasthan for a collection of your works –
I have the honor to be Sir
With great respect
Your very Obliged + Obedient Servt
Wm Huttmann

680
Royal Asiatic Societys House
Grafton Street London
April 20th 1830

Sir

---

151   John Francis Davis: Poeseos sinensis commentarii. On the poetry of the Chinese: read May 2, 1829. *Transaction of the Royal Asiatic Society* 2.1830, 393–461.

I have the pleasure of informing you that the Oriental Translation Committee is quite willing to pay 600 Francs for Mons[r] Titsinghs[152] MS translations of the History of Japan and Remarks on the Chronology of the Chinese and if you will point out the channel through which you wish that sum to be forwarded to you I will remit it immediately

As I think that I have the Japanese original of the remarks on the Chronology of the Chinese I shall be particularly obliged by your favoring me with it at an early opportunity that I may ascertain if it would be worth collating with the original and translating into English

The number of copies of the Annals of Japan that will be wanted is 200 printed on large and fine paper and 500 on smaller and commoner paper – but as the estimate you favored me with is only for 500 copies the paper and press work of the additional 200 will of course be an extra charge

You have I believe several specimens of the quality of the paper and stile of printing adopted by the Committee for the small paper copies and I will forward a large paper copy of the Adventures of Hatim Taï[153] to you as a specimen of the large paper copies – that your translation may correspond in size quality of paper etc. with the Committees other publications

As you wish that some copies of the Annals should remain at Paris for sale on the Committees account 200 of the small paper copies – exclusive of the 25 to which you are entitled for presentation – and the whole of the large paper copies – except one for your own Library for which I will send you an ornamented title – and the remaining 275 small paper copies may be sent to London

I am specially directed by the Committee to request that you will give the most positive orders to the printer not to print more copies of the work than is mentioned above – and the Committee will be particularly obliged by your using your best endeavors to prevent his disobeying your orders – as it is imagined that without your vigilance a considerable number might possibly be clandestinely printed and sold – which would interfere with the sale of the authorisd edition

In relation to the Map – of which you sent a very beautiful specimen which I now return – the Committee has directed me to say – that as the expense of engraving printing and coloring it would be considerable and it is not essentially necessary as an accompaniment to your history – they think that it had better be omitted

After a very long delay and the receipt of a Letter requesting an answer about your Chrestomathie Manchou Messrs Parbury + Co have sent the enclosed reply to your proposed exchange

Colonel Tod has requested me to inform you that he has directed his Bookseller to send a copy of the Rajasthan here for you – I will write to the Bookseller for it this evening and directly it comes will forward it along with Hatim Taï by the Messageries Royales – The Colonel has requested me also to mention that the only copies of your works in his possession are the 1st and 2nd numbers of your Magazin Asiatique – He would also be greatly obliged by your favoring him with the numbers of the Journal Asiatique for Septembre 1829 and Fevrier and Mar 1830 –

I have the honor to be Sir

---

152   Isaac Titsingh (Amsterdam 10. Jan. 1745–2. Febr. 1812 Paris), Kaufmann und Beamter; er trat in den Dienst der Holländischen Ostindien-Kompanie und leitete 1779–1784 die Faktorei auf Deshima (Nagasaki); 1785–1792 war er Generalgouverneur der Kompanie in Bengalen. 1795 unternahm er eine Gesandtschaftsreise nach Peking, mit A. E. van Braam Houckgeest.

153   *The adventures of Hatim Tai.* A romance. Translated from the Persian by Duncan Forbes. London: Oriental Translation Fund, sold by J. Murray 1830. XI, 214 S.

With great respect
Your very Obliged + Obedient Servant
Wm Huttmann

700
London May 1 1830

Sir

I have the honor of returning you the thanks of the Royal Asiatic Society for your Answer to some remarks in Mr Daviss Preface[154] and my personal thank for the copy you obligingly sent for

The other copies have been delivered to the Individuals to whom they were addressd –

I have got Coll Tods Rajasthana – shall I keep it till I get Johnsons Arabic Dictionary or send it by itself? Has Mr Allen informed Parbury + Co of the arrangement he made with you? I have requested Parbury Co to send me a copy for you directly they receive advice of the exchange agreed upon – from Mr. Allen

When you was in London a few years since you collected materials for a Catalogue of the Chinese Books presented to the Royal Asiatic Society by Sir George Staunton If you would lend those materials to me I should consider et a very particular favor as I anxious to make out a Catalogue of the, and your memorandums would be of great assistance to me and save me very much time which is a thing I am often much distressd for
I remain Sir
With great respect
Your very Obliged + Obedient Servt
Wm Huttmann

PS The Bill for 600 francs was of course paid on its presentation

720
Royal Asiatic Societys House
Grafton Street London
May 29 1830

Sir

I had some days since the pleasure of sending a packet to you in which was included a fine paper copy of Hatim Taï as a specimen of the quality of the paper for the Subscribers to the Oriental Translation Fund

The Translation Committee is decidedly of opinion that it is not necessary to send paper from London for the Subscribers copies of the Annals of Japan as they consider that the paper used for printing fine paper copies of works at Paris is quite good enough I shall therefore be obliged by your directing

the Printer to get paper for the Subscribers copies as much like that on which Hatim Taï is printed as he can – but its exactly corresponding with it is not necessary

---

154   Klaproth: Réponse à quelques passages de la préface du roman chinois intitulé: Hao khieo tchhouan, traduit par M. F. Davis. *NJA* 5.1830, 97–114.

I very much regret my inability to send you any copies of the Canton Register as neither Sir George Staunton Mr Marjoribanks nor Mr. Davis receive it and I do not know any other person in London to whom it is likely to be sent

I am extremely obliged by the information about M Paravey[155] which shall be punctually attended to

Should there happen to be a Mandchu Translation of the Tchun tsew of Confucius at Paris for sale I should be extremely obliged by your mentioning it to me and stating its price

Along with Coll Tods Rajasthan Johnsons edition of Richardsons Dictionary etc. I sent you a Japanese work on Chronology – which I shall be obliged by your returning with Titsinghs Treatise on the same subject when you have finished your Annals –

The Committee is – of course – quite willing that the Officers of the imprimerie Royale should have the usual number of copies of your works –

If you should see the Agent to the Societe Asiatique I should be extremely obliged by your mentioning that we are having the Societys copy of the Nouveau Journal Asiatique bound – and find that Numbers 4 - 6 - 10 – 11 and 25 are deficient – If therefore he could favor the Society with those numbers I shall be much obliged –

Hoping that you will pardon my again troubling you with some Letters for the Post
I remain Sir
With Sincere Respect
Your very Obliged + Obedient Serv
Wm Huttmann

740
Royal Asiatic Societys House
Grafton St London
August 18 1830

Dear Sir
I have the pleasure of forwarding to you a copy of the 2nd part of the 2nd Volume of the Transactions of the Royal Asiatic Society

I sincerely hope that recent occurrences at Paris will not retard the publication of your History of Japan as the Oriental Translation Committee in general – and myself in particular – are very anxious to see a sheet of it in print

You would very greatly oblige me by procuring a copy of the Reglemens or Statutes of the Legion of Honour and of any other European orders of Civil Merit

Hoping that you will pardon my troubling you with this request
I remain Dear Sir
With great respect
Your very Obliged + Obedient Serv
Wm Huttmann

Will you oblige me by allowing your Servant to put the accompanying Letters into the Post office?

---

155   Charles Hippolyte de Paravey (Fumay, Ardennes 25. Sept. 1787–1871 St.-Germain-en-Laye), Ingenieur und Orientalist. Vgl. Jean-Claude Drouin: Un esprit original du XIXᵉ siècle: le chevalier de Paravey (1787–1871). *Revue d'histoire de Bordeaux et du département de la Gironde* 1970, 65–78.

750
Royal Asiatic Societys House
Grafton Street London
September 10 1830

Dear Sir
Having copied the collection of laws etc. of the Legion of Honor I haste to return it to you with many thanks for the great trouble you took to obtain it for me –

When you are writing to you [!] – will you oblige me by mentioning the price for which the set of the Moniteur would be sold – and I will then endeavor to find a purchaser

I extremely regret that the confusion at the Imprimerie Royale retards the printing of the Annals of Japan but hope that the delay occasioned by the late occurrences will soon terminate

You have I doubt not observed the correction of the Editor of the Asiatic Journals very stupid blunder about Hwang te – I have also forwarded to him your note relating to the title Bek

Captn Beecheys Voyage is not yet published The accompanying sheets of the Indian Atlas cost 6/s each
I have the honor to be
Dear Sir
With Sincere Respect
Your very Obliged + Obedient Servt
Wm Huttmann

760
Royal Asiatic Societys House
Grafton St London
October 1 1830

Dear Sir
May I presume to ask if you will obligingly arrange with the Editor of Prospectus of the Nouveau Journal Asiatique to have the Report etc. of the Oriental Translation Committee stitched up with that publication – the Committee paying whatever reasonable sum is charged and sending the number of copies that will be wanted for that purpose

When one or two Sheets of your Annals of Japan are printed I should be particularly gratified by being favord with a sight of them
I have the honor to be Dear Sir
Your Sincerely Obliged + Obedient
Wm Huttmann

Monsr J de Klaproth

770
Royal Asiatic Societys House
Grafton St London
October 19 1830

Dear Sir

I am extremely obliged by your kindly arranging to have the Oriental Translation Committees Report etc. stitched up with the Journal Asiatique and will immediately send 400 copies of it to Messrs Treuttell + Würtz with directions to forward them to the Agent of the Societe Asiatique

Supposing that your Annals of Japan were in the Press I placed them among the Books that are being printed – but that is of no consequence as they will soon be in the printers hands

You will I fear consider me very troublesome as I am always asking favors of you – I am now going to request another copy of the 2nd volume of your Memoires as some person has stolen the copy you presented to the Royal Asiatic Society
Assuring you of my gratitude + respect
I remain Dear Sir
Your very Obedient Servant
Wm Huttmann

790
London November 1 1830

Sir

I have received your letters of the 22nd and 25th of October and have summoned a Committee to take them into consideration next Friday when I have no doubt your proposal relative to the large paper for the History of Japan being sent from London will be agreed to – I will communicate the Committees decision to you by that Evenings post

Your Letter to Sir George Staunton was delivered by the Societys porter directly it reached me –

I have again taken the liberty of enclosing some Letters which I hope do not put you to any inconvenience and
I remain Sir
With the greatest Respect
Your very Obliged + Obedient Servt
Wm Huttmann

Monsr Jules de Klaproth

810
London Nov 30 1830
Dear Sir
In compliance with the wish expressd in your Letter of the 26th which I have this moment receivd – I send an official letter relating to the payment of the charge for printing your Annals of Japan which I hope will satisfy the Commissary – If it should not – there would be no difficulty in paying any sum in advance – that he may require

The estimate sent was for 750 copies but the number ordered by the Committee is 500 on small paper und 200 on large paper

You will I hope receive the paper for printing the work upon in a few days –

May I request you will have the packet addressd to Mr de Guignes[156] carefully forwarded to him – as it relates to his fathers MS translation of the Chun tsew – of the existence of which I was not aware until about a week ago

Professor Rosen[157] has requested me to forward to you a copy of his specimen of the Rig Veda and a small parcel for the Societe Asiatique –

Regretting that I am so frequently obliged to lay your kindness under contribution
I remain Dear Sir
Your very Obliged + Obedient Servt
WM Huttmann

820
Royal Asiatic Societys House
Grafton Street London
December 4 1830
7 o'clock p.m.

Dear Sir
Sir George Staunton this morning forwarded to me your letter of the 1st Instant and as the Oriental Translation Committee was sitting when I receivd it I took the liberty of mentioning the subject to them and they agreed to advance the sum you requested on the security of your Library

I regret that the advance was clogged with the condition that your library should be mortgaged to the Committee – but as they are only Trustees of the money subscribed to the Oriental Translation Fund – they did not feel justified in advancing the

money without a tangible security –

On Monday I will pay Twohundred and fifty pounds sterling to Messrs Rothschild & Co to be paid to you through their house at Paris on your delivering to them a deed securing to the Oriental Translation Committee the legal possession of your Library

I will send this Letter to the Foreign Office this Evening – in the hope that a Cabinet Courier may be despatched to Paris before Tuesday – as its early arrival will relieve your anxiety and enable you to have the deed relating to your Library prepared immediately –

Should there be any technical difficulty in legally securing your Library to the Committee – it can be mortgaged to me (as Secretary to the Committee) as a Security for the repayment of the £250

Earnestly hoping that the letter may reach Paris in time to save you from the [1 Zeile gestrichen]
I remain Dear Sir
With great respect
Your very Obedient Servt
Wm Huttmann
Secretary to the Oriental Translation Committee

---

156 Chrétien Louis Joseph de Guignes (25. Aug. 1759–9. März 1845), Kaufmann in China, Dolmetscher und Herausgeber des chinesischen Wörterbuchs von Basilio Brollo in Paris (1813. Vgl. Andreina Albanese: M. de Guignes, un sinologo francese, nella Cina di Qianlong. *Indo-Sino-Tibetica. Studi in onore di Luciano Petech.* Roma: Bardi 1990, 1–24.

157 Friedrich August Rosen (Hannover 2. Sept. 1805–12. Sept. 1837 London), Orientalist und Sanskritist. 1828– 1831 Professor für Orientalistik am University College, London; 1834–1837 Professor für Sanskrit an der Universität London. Vgl. Gregor Pelger: Rosen, Friedrich. *Neue Deutsche Biographie* (NDB). 22.2005, 50–51.

The paper for printing your Annals of Japan will be addressd to the Commissary of the Royal Printing Office Paris

840
London November 5 1830

Sir

I have the pleasure of informing you that the Oriental Translation Committee this afternoon ordered that – in compliance with your wishes – the paper for both the large and small copies of your translation of the annals of Japan should be sent from London it will therefore be forwarded immediately

The number to be printed is large paper 200 – small paper 500 only not 550 –

The letter g in the specimen you sent is not liked by the Committee – could you have the old g substituted for it –

I have enclosed the plates which are missing in your Volume of the Royal Asiatic Societys Transactions and remain Sir
With great respect
Your very Obedient Servant
Wm Huttmann

Monsr Jules de Klaproth

850
London Dec 17. 1830

Dear Sir

I have the pleasure of forwarding to you an open letter addressd to Messr Rothschild which will I hope remove all obstacles to your immediately securing the £250

I have received the deed Mortgaging your Library and should wish it to referrd to in the receipt you give to Messrs Rothschild but if that should be forbidden by the laws of France – I authorise you to place this letter in their hands as their authority for paying you the money on your giving them a common receipt (simple quittance)
I remain Dear Sir
With great respect
Yours very truly
Wm Huttmann

Monsr Jules de Klaproth

870
London Dec. 21. 1830

Dear Sir

I did not receive your Letter announcing that Messrs Rothschild could not pay you the £250 until quite late on Thursday Evening and on Friday Morning I sent a Letter to you enclosing one to them which I doubt not would induce them to pay you that Sum immediately – Should any other difficulty have arisen – which I can scarcely conceive to be possible I beg that you will inform them that I wish the money to be paid to you without further delay or their requiring from you any other receipt that what they are in the habit of taking and you can place the Letter in their hands as their authority for doing so

I very much regret that the Committee required to have your Library mortgaged to them – particularly as it has occasioned so much delay and prolonged your anxiety but as they are only Trustees of the Oriental Translation Fund they felt obliged to require some document to justify them to the Subscribers – and the one you have sent is quite satisfactory –

The whole of the difficulties arose out of my ignorance of the French laws relating to mortgage – as I know that you not possibly surrender your library for two years
Sincerely hoping that all your troubles will be terminated before you receive this Letter
I remain Dear Sir
Your very Obedient Servant
Wm Huttmann
Secretary

880
May I presume to request you will oblige me by having the accompanying Book forwarded to the Jardin des Plantes
Has the paper for printing your Annals of Japan been receivd? It was addressd to the Commissaire of the Imprimerie Royale

890
London January 6. 1831

Sir
I have this day paid into the hands of Messrs Rothschild £62-8-0 and Messrs de Rothschild of Paris will pay 1572 Francs 45 cents to the Cashier of the Royal Printing Office in his sending receipt –

Do you not think that if you was to represent all the circumstances of the transmission of the paper – to the French Government they would remit the duty which appears to be unexpectedly heavy!
I have the honor to be Sir
With great respect
Your very Obedient Servant
Wm Huttmann

Monsieur Jules de Klaproth
Rue d'Amboise, Paris

900
Royal Asiatic Societys House
Grafton Street London
January 11. 1831

Sir

By direction of the Oriental Translation Committee I have the honor of informing you that on the 6th Instant I authorised Messrs de Rothschild of Paris to pay to the Cashier of the Royal Printing Office 1572 Fr 45 c for Custom House duties etc on the paper that was sent from London too print Mr Klaproths Annals of Japan upon – But as the Committee intend applying to the Direction des Douanes for the Remission of the duties – amounting to 1467 f 10 c – which I have no doubt will be granted by a government that has always distinguished itself by its patronage of literature – I am directed to request that you will if possible keep that sum (1467 f 10 c) in your hands until the Committees Petition is decided upon – and should the paper be allowed to be imported free of duty – that sum may remain in your hands as a payment in part for printing the Annals –

There is about 100 francs due for expenses on the paper which Mr Klaproth will obligingly pay to you and I shall reimburse him

Depending on your kind offices in endeavoring to get the paper exempted from the payment of duty
I have the honor to be Sir
With great respect
Your very Obliged + Obedient Servt
Wm Huttmann
Secretary

Monsieur Duvergeur
Commissaire de l'Imprimerie Royale

920
London January 18. 1831

Dear Sir
I have delayed answering your proposal relating to the San Kokf tsou ran[158] until I could submit it to the Oriental Translation Committee – That I have now done and the result is that the Committee is very favorably disposed towards it but wishes to see a specimen of the Maps before deciding on having them lithographed – I shall therefore be obliged by your sending me a copy of one or two of them either in the original or as translated by you –

In relation to the Tsu shu[159] the Committee wish to be favored with a short account of its date + discovery – and some evidence of its authenticity – as there is not any copy of it in London – and it has been suspected of being a fabrication –

I have paid Monsr Metmans draft for 107 f 65 c which balances the account for duties and charges on the paper sent to Paris – but I hope – that he will be allowed to retain in his hands the 1467 f 10 c that are charged for Custom house duties – as I have agreeably with your recommendation – applied for their remission through the British Ambassador at Paris – as you will perceive from the enclosed Letter which I shall be obliged by your

---

158 *Sangoku tsūran zusetsu* 三國通覽圖說 des Hayashi Shihei 林子平 (1738–1793): *San kokf tsou ran to sets, ou Aperçu général des trois royaumes,* traduit de l'original japonais-chinois, par Mr. J. Klaproth. Paris: Oriental Translation Fund; sold by J. Murray 1832. VI, 288 S.
159 nicht identifiziert: 竹書?

sealing and having delivered – The letter is internationally addressd so as to be deliverable either to Lord Stuart or Lord Granville[160]

May I request you to send a copy of the Prospectus of the Christians Magazine which I intend editing – to Galignanis Messenger [161] and any Religious Newspapers and Magazine that are published at Paris –

Hoping that you will pardon the trouble I am constantly giving you

I remain Dear Sir

With great respect

Your very Obliged + Obedient Servt

Wm Huttmann

Monsr Jules de Klaproth, Paris

940

London May 20, 1831

Dear Sir

An unusual press of business – will I hope be accepted as an Apology for my not having replied to your recent Letters earlier

You have I hope receivd Captn Beecheys Voyage[162] – It cost £3.7.0 which I believe is rather more than the balance I had in hand on account of Le Temps – but as I cannot find my statement of the account – if it receives your approbation we will consider than account balanced –

The Oriental Translation Committee has approved of the Charts accompanying your account of Jesso etc. but do not consider it necessary to publish any plates of costumes etc. – and they wish that the Charts should not be given on a very large scale –

The Committee has directed me to express its great satisfaction with the labor and care you have bestowed on the translation of the Annals of Japan – and have desired me to request you to forward a copy of all the sheets that are printed and to continue sending them until after the Annual Meeting which will not take place until about the end of June

I am endeavoring to get a copy of Medhursts Dictionary[163] and if I succeed will do myself the pleasure of presenting it to you

Hoping that you have receivd a packet of Chinese Books lately forwarded to you from Sir George Staunton

I remain Sir

With great respect

Your very Obliged + Obedient Servant

Wm Huttmann

---

160   Lord Granville, d.i. Granville Leveson-Gower (12. Okt. 1773–8. Jan. 1846) war 1804–1805 und 1807–1812 britischer Botschafter in Rußland und 1824–1828, 1830–1835 1835–1841 Botschafter in Frankreich.

161   Giovanni Antonio Galignani (Brescia 1757–1821) founded, in 1814, an English language daily paper *Galignani's Messenger*, in Paris. It flourished but was sold by the family in 1884 when it was continued as *Daily Messenger*.

162   Frederick William Beechey: *Narrative of a voyage to the Pacific and Bering's Strait,* to Co-operate with the Polar Expeditions: Performed in His Majesty's Ship Blossom, under the Command of Captain F. W. Beechey in the Years 1825, 26, 27, 28. London: Colburn & Bentley 1831. 2 Bde.

163   Walter Henry Medhurst: *A dictionary of the Hok-Këèn dialect of the Chinese language*: according to the reading and colloquial Idioms; containing about 12.000 characters ... ; Accompanied by a short historical and statistical account of Hok-këèn. Macao: East India Co.'s Press 1832. LXIV, 860 S.

950
London June 7. 1831

Sir

I hasten to reply to your letter of the 3rd Instant on account of your mentioning that you intend having the Charts for your description of Corea etc. engraved on Copper while it was the intention of the Oriental Translation Committee to have them lithographed as being less than half the expense

As reducing the size would considerably increase the expense of copying it is not of great importance –

If it absolutely necessary for you to draw on me for 400 francs immediately you can do so but it would be better to defer it till after the annual meeting if it will not put you to an inconvenience

The sheets of the great Indian Atlas must have cost me about 6/s each as they are advertised for sale at 8/s each

If the history of Georgia has not been published in French the Oriental Translation Committee will I have no doubt feel willing to publish your translation

Will you be so good as to inform me if the Description of Tibet that you announced some time since is superseded by Pere Hyacinths Translation[164] and should be withdrawn from the List of works preparing for publication by the Oriental Translation Committee –

I am in daily expectation of securing a box of Books from China in which I expect to find the Grammar + probably also the Dictionary of Padre Gonçalves[165] –

When the annual report made to the Societe Asiatique reaches me I will use my influence with the Editor of the Asiatic Journal to give at least an abstract of it in that publication
The title of Colonel FitzClarence is
The Right Honorable the Earl of Munster
and he resides at N° 13 Belgrave Place, Pimlico London
Hoping that you will excuse the hurried manner in which this letter is written
I remain Sir
With great respect
Your very Obedient Servant
Wm Huttmann

PS I am much gratified by learning that you are engaged in a Memoir on the written characters of all nations and hope that it will be accompanied by Specimens of their writing

---

164   Iakinf, Archimandrit (weltlich: Nikita Jakovlevič Bičurin)(27. Aug. 1777–11. Mai 1853), Archimandrit und Sinologe. Er leitete die IX. Geistliche Mission nach Peking (1807–1921), wurde aber wegen zu weltlicher Lebensweise abgesetzt und verbannt, diente dann Baron Schilling von Canstadt auf dessen Reise nach Kjachta und die russisch-chinesischen Grenzgebiete als Dolmetscher und entwickelte sich durch seine Publikationen zu Rußlands führendem Sinologen. Vgl. H. Walravens: *Iakinf Bičurin, russischer Mönch und Sinologe. Eine Biobibliographie.* Berlin: Bell 1988.70 S. (Han-pao tung-Ya shu-chi mu-lu 34.)

165   Joaquim Affonso Gonçalves (23. März 1781–3. Okt. 1844), Geistlicher und Sinologe, vgl. J. M. Callery: Notice biographique sur le père J. A. Gonçalves, comprising an account of his life with notices of his various sinological productions. *Chinese repository* 15.1846, 69–80.

970
London October 1, 1831

Dear Sir
I have the pleasure of informing you that the Oriental Translation Committee has thus day ratified your agreement with Mr. Renouard relative to the printing of the Description of Corea etc.

   I beg you to accept my thanks for the valuable and interesting work on the Physical Geography of Asia to which it is evident you have largely contributed
I have the honor to be Dear Sir
With great respect
Your very Obliged + Obedient Servt
Wm Huttmann

Monsieur Jules de Klaproth
Paris

Namenregister

Die Namen G. T. Staunton, Edward King, William Huttmann und Julius Klaproth sind nicht aufgenommen.

Weitere Bücher desselben Verfassers im Verlag BoD

Carl Graf von Klinckowstroem (1884–1969). Schriftenverzeichnis des Technikhistorikers, Wünschelrutenexperten, Okkultismuskritikers und Bibliophilen.
Norderstedt: BoD 2015. 328 S.
ISBN 978-3.7386-3872-1

Newspapers on the Mind – Around the World. The IFLA Round Table on Newspapers (RTN) 1989 – 2009.
Norderstedt: BoD 2017. 296 S. 4°

Julius Kurth (1870–1949): Briefe an den Dichter Börries von Münchhausen (1874–1945).
Norderstedt: BoD 2017. 135 S.
ISBN 9783746030333

Julius Kurth (1870–1949): „Autogramme" und Fabeln für Börries Frhr. von Münchhausen. Bibliophile Scherze.
Norderstedt: BoD 2017. 99 S.
ISBN 9783746059976

(mit Christine Bell) *Mein inniggeliebter Louis!*
Postkarten an den Elsässer Louis J. Stoffer (1889–1956), Hamburg und Tacoma
Ein Mosaiksteinchen zur Familien- und Auswanderungsgeschichte.
Norderstedt: BoD 2018. 136 S. 4° (zweisprachig)
ISBN 978-3-7460-9487-8

Br. Berchmans Brückner SVD und die *Ars Sacra Pekinensis.* Briefwechsel mit dem Kunsthändler Walter Exner (1911–2003)
Norderstedt: BoD 2018. 166 S. ISBN 9783752820850

Walther Heissig (1913–2005). Aus dem Nachlaß des Mongolisten und Ethnologen – Nachlaßübersicht – Briefwechsel mit Erich Haenisch, Lajos Ligeti, Käthe Uray-Köhalmi, John R. Krueger und Erik Haarh.
Norderstedt: BoD 2018. 219 S. 4°
ISBN 9783748180708

Statehood in the Altaic World. Proceedings of the 59th Annual Meeting of the Permanent International Altaistic Conference (PIAC), Ardahan, Turkey, June 26–July 1, 2016. Norderstedt 2018. ISBN 978-3-7528-0263-4

Johann Redowskys Reise von Irkutsk nach Kamtschatka (1806–1807) im Auftrag der Akademie der Wissenschaften. Das wissenschaftliche Tagebuch des Forschers – Botanik – Geologie – Ethnographie der Jakuten und Tungusen
Norderstedt: BoD 2019. 163 S.
ISBN 9783748188971

George Robert Loehr jr. (1892–1974) und die Forschung über die Pekinger Jesuitenkünstler. Quellen und Materialien in deutscher Sprache
In Verbindung mit Marion Steinicke herausgegeben.
Norderstedt: BoD 2019. 489 S.   ISBN 9783749410705

Walther Heissig: *Aus dem Nachlaß II:*
Briefwechsel mit György Kara, Herbert Franke, György Hazai und Alice Sárközi sowie aus den Anfängen der Altaistenkonferenz (PIAC). – Katalog mongolischer Blockdrucke in London.
Norderstedt: BoD 2019. 217 S.   ISBN 9783739218830

Zur klassischen poetischen Literatur Chinas. Leitfaden zu den Übersetzungen und Rezensionen von Erwin von Zach (1872–1942).
Norderstedt: BoD 2019. 324 S. ISBN 9783741210174

Neue Rückschau auf ein arbeitsreiches Leben. Hartmut Walravens zum 75sten: Thematisches annotiertes Schriftenverzeichnis. Mit Einleitung und Registern.
Bibliographie – Bibliotheken – Zeitungen – Erotica – Normung – China – Japan –Altaistik – Mandschurei – Mongolei – Tibet – Rußland.
Norderstedt: BoD 2019. 236 S.   ISBN 9783748108610

Verzeichnis der Veröffentlichungen von Professor Dr. Martin Gimm.
Norderstedt: BoD 2020. 48 S. 4° ISBN 978-3-7431-6665-3

Franz Blei (1871–1942), Carl Georg von Maassen (1880–1940) und Hans von Müller (1875–1944) im Briefwechsel. Auch ein Mosaiksteinchen zur E. T. A. Hoffmann-Forschung.
Norderstedt: BoD 2020. 168 S. ISBN 978-3-7504-9525-8

Jean Pierre Abel Rémusat (1788–1832). Zu Leben und Werk eines Wegbereiters der Ostasienwissenschaften. Norderstedt: BoD 2020. 153 S. ISBN 978-3-7519-3088-8

Julius Klaproths (1783–1835) Briefe an den Orientalisten und Erfinder Paul Ludwig Schilling von Canstadt (1786–1837). Samt Schreiben an den Sinologus Berolinensis sowie Ergänzungen zum Schriftenverzeichnis Klaproths.
Norderstedt: BoD 2020. 100 S. 4° ISBN 978-3-7519-8420-1

(mit Albert König:) *Roter und gelber Papagei (Ara macao und Psittacula krameri, gelbe Mutation) am Kaiserhof in Peking.*
Norderstedt: BoD 2020. 44 S. 4° ISBN 978-3-7526-2644-5

[Hrsg.] *Der Traum meines ganzen Lebens: Die epochale Amerika-Reise Alexander von Humboldts.*
Norderstedt: BoD 2021. 274 S. ISBN 978-3-7526-8932-7

Stanislas Julien (1797–1873): Wissenschaftliche Korrespondenz über China mit Schilling von Canstadt, Klaproth, Endlicher, Gabelentz, und A. von Humboldt.
Norderstedt: BoD 2021. 110 S. ISBN 978-3-7526-4182-0

Books on Demand (BoD)
In de Tarpen 42, 22848 Hamburg
Tel.: +49 (0)40 53 43 35 11
EMail: info@bod.de